Grade **6**

Scott Foresman

# The Grammar & Writing Book

ISBN 13: 978-0-328-11801-4
ISBN 10: 0-328-11801-X

Copyright © Pearson Education, Inc.
All Rights Reserved. Printed in the United States of America. This publication is protected by Copyright, and permission should be obtained from the publisher prior to any prohibited reproduction, storage in a retrieval system, or transmission in any form by any means, electronic, mechanical, photocopying, recording, or likewise. For information regarding permission(s), write to: Permissions Department, Scott Foresman, 1900 East Lake Avenue, Glenview, Illinois 60025.

6 7 8 9 10 V008 16 15 14 13 12 11 10 09 08 07

CC1

PEARSON

Scott
Foresman

Editorial Offices: Glenview, Illinois • Parsippany, New Jersey • New York, New York
Sales Offices: Boston, Massachusetts • Duluth, Georgia • Glenview, Illinois
Coppell, Texas • Sacramento, California • Mesa, Arizona

# Table of Contents

## Writer's Guide

## Rubrics and Models

## Evaluate Your Writing

## Grammar and Writing Lessons

# Writing for Tests

# Grammar Patrol

# Index

# Writer's Guide

# Focus/Ideas

> Good writers **focus** on a **main idea** and develop this idea with strong, supporting details. In addition, they know their purpose for writing. This purpose may be to persuade, to inform, to describe, or to entertain. Your purpose is important because it helps you focus on your main idea.

Even a postcard has a main idea and a purpose.

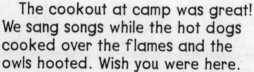

Dear Lee,
    The cookout at camp was great! We sang songs while the hot dogs cooked over the flames and the owls hooted. Wish you were here.
                                        Best,
                                        Craig

**Main Idea**  Craig is enjoying camp.

**Purpose**  To inform Lee

**Details**  This postcard gives Lee a glimpse of camp life. Details make the writing lively. Compare these two sentences:

- Camp is busy and fun. (dull, with few details)
- We hike in the green hills, paddle aluminum kayaks, and rehearse for the camp musical. (adds color and information)

## Strategies for Focus and Ideas

- Choose a topic that you can handle. For example, "The History of Pennsylvania" is too large a topic for a brief essay.
- Let your purpose fit the topic. For example, a funny story is entertaining; a comparison/contrast of two movies is informative.

**2**  Writer's Guide

**A** Write the letter of the purpose that best suits each numbered writing assignment.

**A** To entertain    **B** To inform    **C** To persuade

1. A letter convincing parents to let you go to camp
2. A set of instructions for assembling a model plane
3. A report on Egypt's pyramids
4. A story about a cat and dog detective team
5. Arguments for having a longer school year

**B** Read the paragraph below. Write the numbers of the sentences that do not focus on the main idea in the first sentence.

**Main idea** By following a few simple steps, you can make perfect pasta. **(6)** First, choose a large pot, fill it two-thirds full of water, and heat it over a burner. **(7)** Add a half teaspoon of salt and a tablespoon of oil. **(8)** When the water begins to boil rapidly, put in the pasta. **(9)** There are many kinds of pasta. **(10)** I like rotini best. **(11)** Stir the pasta every minute or so. **(12)** After it has cooked for 9 minutes, pour the pasta and water into a colander in the sink. **(13)** Drain the pasta, pour it into a bowl, add butter, and enjoy!

**C** Read the details about unusual vegetables below. Write a main idea sentence based on these details. Then write a paragraph using the details.

**Details**   rutabaga—like a cross between a turnip and a squash; yellow and mild

Jerusalem artichoke—crunchy, slightly sweet; a little like potato; actually the root of a sunflower

tomatillo—small, green, sticky; looks like tomato; comes from Mexican ground cherry

# Improving Focus/Ideas

## Original

This is about fast food. I love burgers, fries, pizza, and all that stuff. I could eat it every day. People are busy and don't want to wait for their food, plus fast food tastes great. Tasty Burger is my favorite place.

Fast food is bad for you. I guess burgers and fries have lots of fat. Soft drinks are full of sugar. I drink a couple every day usually. You could order other stuff, like a chicken sandwich or chili. I read that they have a lot less fat.

Fast-food restaurants have new stuff on the menu. There are different salads like this one has chicken and nuts and oranges in it. I'd rather have a burger to tell the truth. Now what to drink. I really want that soft drink, but I could get milk instead. Oh, well. Now that I have been so good, I deserve a hot fudge sundae. Ha!

## Revising Tips

**Write a specific, clear main idea statement.** You could write a strong, focused statement about eating healthy meals at fast-food restaurants.

**Include only details that focus on and develop the main idea.** Delete details that are off the topic. (For example, delete sentences about favorite restaurants and foods.)

**Include enough details to support important points.** Provide specific details about healthy and unhealthy fast foods. (For example, explain which fast foods are bad for you and why.)

**Write a conclusion that reinforces your main idea.** Add an ending that ties together all your points about the main idea.

## Improved

We know that too much fat and sugar are bad for us. But we often have to eat fast, and we love our burgers and fries. Unfortunately, they are full of fat. The soft drinks that go with them are full of sugar. Is there a way to eat healthy meals at a fast-food restaurant? If we can change our habits, the answer is yes.

First, replace that burger with a food lower in fat. For example, try a grilled chicken sandwich or some chili. Both those choices are tasty and low in fat. Many fast-food restaurants are now offering salads and even fresh fruit. These are very healthy choices. Replace the soft drink with milk or water.

Congratulations! Now you are making healthy choices. Please don't reward yourself with a giant ice cream. If you need a treat, get a low-fat yogurt cone. Your body will thank you.

# Writer's Corner

Beware of interesting but irrelevant details. Once you write a clear main idea statement, check all your details against it. If a detail does not relate directly to your main idea, it does not belong.

# Organization/Paragraphs

Every piece of writing needs some kind of **organization.**
The structure is like the frame of a house. It holds everything
together and gives a shape to ideas and details.

Here are some ways to organize your writing:
- a narrative with a beginning, middle, and end
- a step-by-step set of instructions
- a comparison/contrast of two people, places, or things
- a description of something from left to right
- an explanation of causes and effects
- a persuasive piece with the best reason last

Before you write, consider how to best shape your ideas. For example, if
you are explaining how to build a gingerbread house, a set of instructions
would work. If you are sharing a personal experience, a narrative is the
form to use.

Deciding on the form of your writing is just the first step. Consider how
all of your ideas connect to the topic. What organization would best
present your ideas?

## Strategies for Organizing Ideas

- Create a graphic organizer such as a web, outline, chart, or sketch.
- Order steps from first to last.
- Introduce characters, set the scene, and show action.
- Save the most important idea until last and build up to it.
- Use sequence words such as *first, later,* and *now.*
- Use signal words such as *both* and *neither* to show comparisons.

**A** Write the letter of the kind of organization that each numbered writing assignment calls for.

   **A** Description
   **B** Comparison/contrast
   **C** Persuasive argument
   **D** Set of instructions
   **1.** Tell how twin sisters are alike and different.
   **2.** Create a vivid word picture of a wolf.
   **3.** List the steps in making lemonade.
   **4.** Convince parents to buy you a computer.

**B** A description often presents details about an object from top to bottom or left to right. Read the following paragraph describing a mountain. Choose a detail about location from the box that best fits each sentence. Rewrite the paragraph.

| | |
|---|---|
| around the base of the mountain | above the clouds |
| where the slopes grew steeper | above the forest line |
| on the gentle slopes near the base | into swirls of white cloud |

   **(5)** ____, farmland spread out and cattle grazed. **(6)** ____, herds of sheep walked among the wildflowers. **(7)** Higher up, ____, evergreen forests grew. **(8)** Rocky cliffs rose sheer ____. **(9)** The cliffs seemed to disappear ____. **(10)** The ice-covered peak rose like a spearhead ____.

**C** Write a paragraph explaining the causes of a problem such as pollution or erosion. Suggest a possible solution. Use words such as *so, as a result,* and *because* to show how ideas are related.

# Improving Organization/Paragraphs

## Original

> It is time to write another book report, and book reports are not my favorite thing. They are kind of boring because we always write the same kind of information.
>
> One thing that would be more fun would be if we acted out scenes from books. Or we could write songs or have talk shows about our books' characters.
>
> The class is getting bored with writing the same old reports. Aren't book reports supposed to make us want to read? Bored students are turned off to reading. Cool projects would be fun and exciting. Everyone would remember a play or a song based on a book. Writing is not the best way for everyone to learn.
>
> Special projects would be entertaining. I think we would remember the books better and want to read more. That's all.

## Revising Tips

**Begin with a clear statement of your main idea.** Focus on the problem and how you think it should be solved.

**Organize your support logically in well-developed paragraphs.** State reasons why your solution or opinion is best, one at a time, and develop them with supporting details.

**Use transition words and phrases to show how ideas are connected.** Introduce reasons with *first, also,* and *most important.* End with the strongest reason.

**Tie ideas together in your conclusion.** Avoid an abrupt ending. Refer back to your main idea, using different wording.

## Improved

It is time to write another book report, and I have the book report blues. I'd like to propose a change to get rid of those blues. Instead of writing the same old book reports, why don't we make special projects about the books we read?

There are several reasons to make a change. First, the class is getting bored with writing the same old reports. Aren't book reports supposed to make us want to read? Bored students are turned off to reading. Second, cool projects would entertain us. Everyone would enjoy a play or a song based on a book.

It is also true that writing is not necessarily the best way for everyone to learn. We could share our books by acting out scenes or having a talk show for the characters in the books.

Most important, students would remember the books better and want to read more because they would use their imaginations in a fun way. Let's get started today and brainstorm ideas for fun book projects!

## Writer's Corner

Make a "ladder" and summarize your main argument at the top and your reasons on the rungs. Be sure each rung below the main statement states a new reason. The final rung should tell the most important reason.

Treasure Island

# Voice

Every writer has a **voice**—a personality that comes through in the tone and style of a piece of writing. Voice shows that a writer knows and cares about a topic. It also reveals a certain style and tone. A writer with a strong, clear voice speaks directly to readers and keeps their attention.

- I stood on the bridge and looked at the water. (weak voice)
- I leaned over the railing of the bridge, scowling down at the muddy, brown waters of the river. (strong voice)

Voice should take into account what the reader needs to know. Your topic, audience, and purpose will determine your voice.

## Strategies for Developing Your Voice

- Be sure of your purpose and audience. A review of a school play that flopped might have a humorous, light voice. An argument for more lifeguards at the town beach demands a serious, thoughtful voice.
- Select words that match your voice. When you write dialogue for characters in a story, you can use contractions *(I've, it's)* along with slang. Figurative language can make your voice interesting and colorful. Formal writing, such as research reports and business letters, requires exact, objective vocabulary.
- Remember that your voice shapes and controls your ideas. Whatever you write about, express yourself in an engaging, appropriate voice.

**A** Write the letter of the type of writing that would include each numbered topic sentence.

> **A** Personal narrative  **C** Business report
> **B** Book review  **D** Comparison/contrast essay

1. We expect excellence from the creator of Harry Potter, and with her newest book, J. K. Rowling does not disappoint us.
2. Swimming in the ocean is nothing like swimming in a lake.
3. The student council began the year with $187.50 in the treasury.
4. When the tornado warning sirens sounded, my mom took charge.

**B** Some sentences in the business letter below have a "voice problem." Write the letter of each problem next to the number of the sentence that has that problem. Write *D* if the sentence has no voice problem.

> **A** Slang  **C** Inappropriate humor
> **B** Too formal  **D** No voice problem

 (5) Our club has received your bill for the chocolate bars we ordered for our fundraiser. (6) According to this bill, you shipped us 5,000 bars and we owe you $3,500. (7) No way! You are so out of line! (8) Do you think we are a bunch of chocolate junkies? Ha! (9) Our records show that we ordered 1,000 bars at a total cost of $750. (10) We shall delay payment until you adjust our bill.

**C** Complete the statement below. Then develop the idea with at least five sentences, using a humorous, light voice.

 The most hilarious thing I ever saw was _____.

# Improving Voice

## Original

Last night there was a raccoon in the yard. Raccoons are wild animals that have gray-brown fur and a striped tail and a black stripe across their eyes that looks like a mask. I was surprised to see him. He stood on his back legs and looked at me.

He must have figured I wasn't an enemy because he got down in the grass and got himself some birdseed. There is a bird feeder in the yard and birds scatter the seed on the ground under it. I didn't know a raccoon would eat birdseed. It sounds gross.

He must have liked it, for he kept eating for a long time. Then he turned without giving me a second glance and walked off.

## Revising Tips

**Establish a voice in the opening paragraph.** Create a voice that establishes your mood and your feeling for the subject.

**Use interesting language to suggest your personality and get your reader involved.** Replace flat, dull sentences with vivid ones that bring the topic to life.

**Elaborate on your ideas. Use precise, descriptive details rather than vague, general ones.** (Replace *got himself some birdseed* with *scrabbled around in the grass under the bird feeder and expertly raked in the seeds scattered by birds*.)

**Match your language to your purpose.** Don't use slang or overly informal words in a personal narrative. (Replace *It sounds gross*.)

## Improved

Last night a masked bandit surprised me in the yard. The raccoon was surprised too and reared up on his hind legs to get a good look at me. With that black stripe across his face, he looked like a stubby-legged pirate with a thick furry cape wrapped around his wide body. He spread his paws as if to say, "Well? And what do you want? Are we okay here?"

He must have decided I wasn't an enemy because he went back to his business. His business was dinner. He scrabbled around in the grass under the bird feeder and expertly raked in the seeds scattered by birds. When he had a nice little pile, he leaned forward to chomp it down. "Ugh!" I thought, as I imagined swallowing the hard slivers of grain and seeds.

Still, it must have suited him fine, for he kept at it a long time. Then he turned without giving me a second glance and ambled off, waving his bushy, striped tail like a flag.

## Writer's Corner

Your attitude toward your subject comes through your voice; before you begin writing, consider how you feel about your topic. Allow those feelings to guide your choice of words. They should reflect your personality and attitude and also create a suitable tone for the subject.

# Word Choice

Good writers always search for the perfect **words** to express an idea. Precise nouns, strong verbs, and vivid adjectives make their writing unforgettable.

- London is an example of a foggy city and is covered with thick clouds much of the time. (dull and wordy)
- London's fog is a fine mist that blankets its streets and chills its citizens. (vivid and precise)

## Strategies for Improving Word Choice

- Appeal to the senses. *(The elephant's hide was cracked like dry earth* instead of *The elephant's skin looked dry; The moon hangs like a pearl earring* instead of *The moon is white and round)*
- Use precise nouns. *(heron* instead of *bird; skyscraper* instead of *building)*
- Harness the power of strong verbs. *(whisper* instead of *say; galloped* instead of *ran)*
- Eliminate wordiness. *(I believe* instead of *It is my opinion that)*
- Banish empty words—*good, cute, stuff, nice.* Choose words with meaning. *(The cellar held battered trunks, rusted lawnmowers, and countless cardboard boxes* instead of *The cellar was full of stuff)*
- Try rewriting sentences that depend on linking verbs—*is, am, were. (The bell jangled in my ears* instead of *The bell was loud)*
- Find words that make magic on the page: *shadowy, harsh, glimmer, devastated.* Jot these words down in a writer's notebook for future reference.

**A** Choose the more vivid or exact word or phrase to complete each sentence. Write the sentence.

1. Bev (sat, slumped) in her chair and sighed.
2. The hours (passed, trickled by) slowly.
3. When the bell rang, she (rocketed, walked) to her locker.
4. (An avalanche, A bunch) of books fell when she opened the door.
5. She slammed the door shut on that (chaotic, messy) locker.
6. At last, spring break had (freed her from confinement, started).

**B** Replace the underlined word in each sentence with a more exact word or phrase from the box. Rewrite the paragraph.

| | | |
|---|---|---|
| threatening | bucked | roar |
| cracked | torrents | fresh as dawn |

(7) We could hear the storm <u>come</u> in from the west. (8) Trees <u>moved</u> violently as wind whipped them. (9) <u>Black</u> clouds had suddenly filled the sky. (10) Then <u>lots</u> of rain fell in windblown sheets. (11) I jumped as lightning ripped the sky and thunder <u>sounded</u> like a gunshot. (12) Afterwards, the air smelled <u>good</u>.

**C** Write a description of a runner in a race. Use precise nouns, strong verbs, and vivid adjectives to make your writing powerful.

# Improving Word Choice

## Original

Paul saw something, and it surprised him. He stepped back into the shadows. Something was walking across his sleeping bag. What on Earth was it? Or was it from Earth?

It was kind of round and flat, sort of like a spaceship. It had a face sticking out one end. It was covered with the weirdest stuff—not exactly fur or skin, more like needles.

It stood still when he made the noise. Then it turned around and was looking at him. Paul was nervous, but he was curious too. He went forward. The thing made a weird noise.

"Would you look at that!" said a voice behind Paul. The thing left. Paul found out from Mr. Bowie it was a hedgehog.

## Revising Tips

**Replace vague or general nouns.** Substitute the names of specific people, places, or things. (Use *spines* instead of *stuff*.)

**Use vivid verbs to describe actions precisely.** (Replace *walking* with *padding*; replace *stood still* with *froze*; replace *said* with *exclaimed*.)

**Elaborate with words that appeal to the senses.** (Use *hissed* instead of *made a weird noise*.)

**Use images and figurative language to create strong word pictures.** (Use *like a pincushion* instead of *more like needles*.)

**Avoid wordiness.** Rewrite sentences that contain unnecessary words. (Delete *kind of* and *sort of*.)

## Improved

Paul gasped and automatically stepped back into the shadows. A bizarre creature was padding across his sleeping bag. What on Earth was it? Or WAS it from Earth?

Its body was rounded, like a weird, warped flying saucer. The only indication that it had a front was a tiny, sharp muzzle extending from one end. It was covered with thousands of sharp spines that rustled against one another. "Like a pincushion," muttered Paul.

The pincushion/flying saucer froze at the sound. Then it whirled to face him. With his heart in his throat, the curious boy inched forward. The creature hissed.

"Would you look at that!" exclaimed a deep voice from over Paul's left shoulder. While the creature waddled away, Paul learned from Mr. Bowie that he had just seen his first hedgehog.

## Writer's Corner

Figurative language can make your writing come alive. Consider whether you might describe your subject more vividly by using a figurative comparison, such as the "pincushion" simile used above for the hedgehog.

# Sentences

> Good writing has a natural flow. **Sentences** that vary in structure and length create a readable style. When writing follows the rhythms of speech, it is a pleasure to read aloud.

Here are some ways to improve your sentences.

- Vary sentence types. Use interrogative, exclamatory, and imperative sentences along with declarative sentences.
- Write sentences of varying lengths.
- Begin sentences with words other than *the, I,* or *it.*
- Use connectors. Show relationships between ideas with words such as *although, but, next, while,* and *however.* Don't rely too heavily on *and, so,* and *because.*

## Strategy for Improving Your Sentences

Reread a piece of your writing and number each sentence. Then make a chart like the one below and examine each sentence.

| Sentence number | Number of words | First word | Type of sentence (Interrogative, Declarative, Imperative, Exclamatory) | Connector words |
|---|---|---|---|---|

As you fill out your chart, look for areas to improve. You may learn that you overuse *but* or *and* to connect ideas. Maybe your sentences could be longer and more varied. When you revise your writing, improve these areas.

**A** Use the connector in ( ) to join each pair of sentences. Write the new sentences. Use commas as needed.

1. Everyone likes barbecue. ____ People in different regions prepare it in different ways. (although)

2. ____ We make barbecued ribs. Dad rubs them with a mixture of spices. (when)

3. Some people season their barbecue with vinegar and pepper. ____ Others baste it with sweet tomato sauce. (while)

4. ____ I eat barbecue. My fingers and cheeks are sticky with sauce. (after)

5. It is a messy treat. ____ It is so delicious that I don't mind the mess. (but)

**B** In the paragraph below, change each sentence to the kind of sentence indicated in ( ). Write the paragraph. Hint: Begin the exclamatory sentences with *What*.

(6) I made a mess when I baked a cake. (exclamatory) (7) Picture what happens when you take the mixer out of the batter without turning off the mixer. (interrogative) (8) You can imagine batter all over the walls and ceiling. (imperative) (9) All that batter could be in one bowl. (interrogative) (10) I made a tiny cake. (exclamatory)

**C** Write a description of your favorite food. Use all four kinds of sentences. Vary sentence lengths, and begin each sentence with a different word.

# Improving Sentences

## Original

I love Fourth of July at our home. I think it is so much fun. I like how the day begins with a beehive of activity. We set up tables in the yard. Then we set up chairs around them. We put a centerpiece with flowers and flags in the center of the tables. We get out the festive red, white, and blue plates. We start the grill.

Guests begin arriving and they walk up the driveway and they sniff the air hungrily. You can smell hot dogs and hamburgers cooking. We have a wonderful feast. I especially like the potato salad. Everybody anticipates the fireworks to come.

Kids play croquet in the shade. Some kids change into swimsuits and play on the Slip 'n Slide. I can slide 50 feet on it.

Now it is getting dark. We sit facing the park with anticipation. Everyone is waiting. Now the fireworks begin exploding. They look like huge flowers in the night sky.

## Revising Tips

**Vary sentence beginnings.** Avoid starting too many sentences with *I* and *we.*

**Join short, choppy sentences.** Use connectors such as *and, or, as,* and *while* to join sentences with related ideas.

**Avoid sentences that are too long or wordy.** (Break the first sentence in the second paragraph into two sentences.)

**Order sentences for a logical flow.** (Move information about anticipating fireworks from the second paragraph to the last paragraph.)

**Vary kinds and lengths of sentences.** Rephrase some statements as exclamations, questions, or commands.

## Improved

Fourth of July is a special day at our home. Won't you join us? The day begins with a beehive of activity as we set up tables and chairs in the yard. A centerpiece with flowers and flags goes in the center of each table. Mom gets out the festive red, white, and blue dinnerware while Dad fires up the grill.

Soon guests begin arriving. As they walk up, they sniff the air hungrily. Can you smell the hot dogs and hamburgers cooking? Pass me some of that potato salad, please. What a wonderful feast we have!

Kids play croquet in the shade or change into swimsuits and play on the Slip 'n Slide. Did you know I can slide 50 feet on that wet plastic?

Now it is getting dark, and we sit facing the park with anticipation. Boom! The fireworks begin exploding like huge flowers in the night sky.

## Writer's Corner

Avoid running several sentences together with the conjunction *and*. The result is a long train of ideas that all seem of equal importance. Instead, use connectors such as *when* and *before* to show relationships. Eliminate unnecessary words.

*No:*   School let out and I visited my aunt and she lives in Georgia.

*Yes:*   When school let out, I visited my aunt in Georgia.

# Conventions

Conventions are rules for written language. They are the signals that writers use to make their meaning clear to readers. For example, sentences begin with a capital letter and end with punctuation. Paragraphs are indented to show where a new idea begins. Grammar and spelling follow patterns.

- sam and he frens walkd to the stor they buyed ice creem (weak conventions)

- Sam and his friends walked to the store. They bought ice cream. (strong conventions)

## Strategies for Conventions of Writing

- Make sure sentences are complete, with correct capitalization and punctuation.
- Use a dictionary or spell-checker to check spelling.
- Choose the correct forms of pronouns, especially pronouns that are compound subjects or objects.
- Do not change verb tenses without a reason.
- Check the use of apostrophes in possessive nouns and contractions.
- Use Proofreading Marks as you revise and edit your work.

## Proofreading Marks

 New paragraph

 Capital letter

 Lowercase letter

 Correct the spelling.

 Add something.

 Remove something.

**A** Match the letter of the rule with the mistake in each numbered sentence.

    **A** Capitalize a proper noun.

    **B** Change a capital letter to lowercase.

    **C** Correct a misspelled word.

    **D** Use correct end punctuation.

    **E** Use the correct pronoun form.

    **(1)** I am hoping to try out for the sabers, the junior high school soccer team. **(2)** My older Brother Darius plays on the team now. **(3)** I watch he and his friend practice to pick up pointers. **(4)** He asked if I was ready to run five miles in practice? **(5)** You have to be in grate shape to play a whole soccer game.

**B** Choose the correct word from each pair in ( ). Write the word.

    **6.** (Their, There) are many ways to get exercise.

    **7.** I (like, likes) swimming best.

    **8.** Jimmy told Val and (I, me) that he runs daily.

    **9.** Some people think (its, it's) hard to find time for exercise.

    **10.** As for me, I have never (saw, seen) an activity I didn't like.

**C** Write six sentences about one of the topics below. Think carefully about spelling, grammar, punctuation, and capitalization. Exchange papers with a partner and proofread.

- How you feel about being active
- Your TV watching habits
- A game that you played

# Improving Conventions

## Original

> Every august our town celebrates CornFest this three-day festival draws people from miles around and sets the whole county abuzz with nosie and activity.
>
> The downtown are closed to traffic, and restaurants opens outdoor stands. The smelles of chinese, Mexican, Italian, and Thai food mingle. Clothing stores wheel out merchandize for sidewalk sales.
>
> A big parking lot hosts carnival rides. Little kids shout and hold on tight as the merry-go-round whirls. I always ride the Ferris wheel and look over the hole town.
>
> Best of all, thousands of people line up for the free sweet corn. Volunteers hand out plates of the steaming treat. The golden ears has been cooked in a huge old steem locomotive boiler.

## Revising Tips

**Do not run sentences together incorrectly.** (Add a period after *CornFest* and capitalize *this* in the first paragraph.)

**Make sure that subjects and verbs agree.** (*downtown is* instead of *downtown are*; *restaurants open* instead of *restaurants opens*; *ears have* instead of *ears has*)

**Spell all words correctly.** (*noise, merchandise, whole,* and *steam* instead of *nosie, merchandize, hole,* and *steem*)

**Capitalize all proper nouns and adjectives.** (*August* and *Chinese* instead of *august* and *chinese*)

**Form plurals of nouns correctly.** (*smells* instead of *smelles*)

## Improved

Every August our town celebrates CornFest. This three-day festival draws people from miles around and sets the whole county abuzz with noise and activity.

The downtown is closed to traffic, and restaurants open outdoor stands. The smells of Chinese, Mexican, Italian, and Thai food mingle. Clothing stores wheel out merchandise for sidewalk sales.

A big parking lot hosts carnival rides. Little kids shout and hold on tight as the merry-go-round whirls. I always ride the Ferris wheel and look over the whole town.

Best of all, thousands of people line up for the free sweet corn. Volunteers hand out plates of the steaming treat. The golden ears have been cooked in a huge old steam locomotive boiler.

## Writer's Corner

When you proofread, try using a ruler. Place the ruler under one line. Read that line carefully from start to finish. Then move the ruler down to the next line. Some people even read backward to catch spelling errors.

# Rubrics and Models

## Narrative Writing *Scoring Rubric*

A scoring **rubric** can be used to judge a piece of writing. A rubric is a checklist of traits, or writing skills, to look for. See pages 2–25 for a discussion of these traits. Rubrics give a number score for each trait.

| Score | 4 | 3 | 2 | 1 |
|---|---|---|---|---|
| **Focus/Ideas** | Excellent narrative focused on a clear main idea; much elaboration | Good narrative mostly focused on a main idea; some elaboration | Unfocused narrative with unrelated details | Rambling narrative with unrelated details |
| **Organization/ Paragraphs** | Strong beginning, middle, and end, with appropriate order words | Narrative movement from beginning to end; some order words | Little direction from beginning to end, with few order words | Lacks beginning, middle, end; incorrect or no order words |
| **Voice** | Writer involved— personality evident | Reveals personality at times | Little writer involvement, personality | Careless writing with no feeling |
| **Word Choice** | Vivid, precise words that bring story to life | Accurate and sometimes vivid word choice | Few vivid or interesting words | Vague, dull, or misused words |
| **Sentences** | Excellent variety of sentences; natural rhythm | No serious errors to affect understanding | Simple, awkward, or wordy sentences; little variety | Many errors that prevent understanding |
| **Conventions** | Excellent control; few or no errors | No serious errors to affect understanding | Weak control; enough errors to affect understanding | Many errors that prevent understanding |

Following are four models that respond to a prompt. Each model has been given a score, based on the rubric.

**Writing Prompt** Write about the scariest event you have ever seen. Be sure your narrative has a beginning, middle, and end. Use vivid words to help readers see and feel what you experienced.

## Narrative Writing Model *Score 4*

Last summer, while hiking on Mount Neeweeshaw, I walked into a waking nightmare. My dad and I stopped to rest. It was scorching, so I wandered over to sit in the shade of a boulder.

Then I heard a strange buzzing. A warning bell went off in my head. Danger is near! My heart thumped like a wild rabbit, but I didn't move a muscle. Moving just my eyes, I could see a shape like a coil of rope. It was a big snake! I knew by the diamond pattern on its back and the rattles at the end of its tail that I was in trouble. The rattler was warning, "I will strike!"

Sweat ran down my arms and legs. I wanted like crazy to run away, but somehow I made myself sit still. Finally, the snake slithered off. The danger had passed, but I was still shaking.

**Focus/Ideas**   Details focused on writer's terrified reaction

**Organization/Paragraphs**   Strong beginning, middle, and end; connectors clarify sequence, cause and effect *(so, then, finally)*

**Voice**   Writer's personal involvement clear *(warning bell went off in my head, heart thumped like a wild rabbit)*

**Word Choice**   Exact nouns *(boulder, rattler)*, strong verbs *(thumped, slithered)*, vivid adjectives *(scorching, diamond)*

**Sentences**   Good sentence variety; mimics natural speech

**Conventions**   No errors

# Narrative Writing Model *Score 3*

The day we went to Mall of America, I was so excited. I love shopping, but things got a little to exciteing.

I went into a shoe store while my mom looked in a gift store. After a while I walked out but nothing looked familiar. Mom was nowhere to be seen. I had this sinking feeling in my stomach. I was lost and I didn't know anyone. Who would help me? I felt a lump in my throat but I swallowed it and went to an information desk. The woman was calm and kind. She made a announcement over the mall intercom. Mom was soon there.

It turned out, I had walked out of the store on another level. The store has two floors.

**Focus/Ideas**   Details mostly support main idea of getting lost in the mall

**Organization/Paragraphs**   Events in order; few connecting words *(After a while)*; weak ending

**Voice**   Writer's feelings clear *(was so excited; sinking feeling)*

**Word Choice**   Some words too general *(went, got)*; *be* verbs overused

**Sentences**   Clear sentences; some variety; too many sentences begin with *I*

**Conventions**   Some errors in spelling *(to, exciteing)*; a usage error *(a announcement)*; punctuation errors (commas needed in compound sentences)

# Narrative Writing Model *Score 2*

> Sarah and me went trick or treating one Halloween. We always go together. She wore karate stuff and I was an army guy. We desided to go to the old Purdy place. Everybody says its haunted. Its been emtee for years. So it was real dark. It used to be a manshen, but it looks bad now. Sarah dare me to go in the house so I did. I hear something moan so I ran out. I was real scared. Then we went to my house. We played video games. I still think somebody was in that house.

**Focus/Ideas**   Weak focus on event; some unrelated details (*We always... We played video games*); little elaboration

**Organization/Paragraphs**   Events mostly in order; wanders off track at times; lacks paragraphing

**Voice**   Little sense of personality; some feelings expressed (*I was real scared*)

**Word Choice**   General, dull words (*went, go, stuff, bad*); overuse of forms of *be*; a few vivid words (*dare, moan*)

**Sentences**   No variety of kinds or lengths; style overly simple; overused connector *so*

**Conventions**   Misspellings (*desided, emtee, manshen, its* instead of *it's*); errors in grammar (*me* instead of *I*); shifts in tense (*dare* and *hear* instead of *dared* and *heard*)

## Narrative Writing Model *Score 1*

We went to the park I like the rides. We usually go every summer. so we drove in the van and Carla and me were watching a DVD so we got there and parked. We got on the roler coster that was the first time it was after lunch. it goed so fast but slow uphill. I culdn't breth I was so scard. never agin I said. but it was fun kind of

**Focus/Ideas**   No main idea stated; most details do not focus on assigned topic; confused

**Organization/Paragraphs**   Events out of order; no paragraphs

**Voice**   Little sense of writer's personality

**Word Choice**   Limited, dull word choice *(went, like, go, got, was)*

**Sentences**   Many run-on sentences; disjointed

**Conventions**   Errors in capitalization, spelling *(roler coster, culdn't, breth, scard, agin)*, verb usage *(goed)*, pronoun usage *(Carla and me)*, and punctuation *(never agin…kind of)*

# Descriptive Writing *Scoring Rubric*

| Score | 4 | 3 | 2 | 1 |
|---|---|---|---|---|
| **Focus/Ideas** | Excellent description with clear main idea and vivid, elaborated details | Good description with adequate details focused on main idea | Some descriptive details; some focus on main idea | Little focus on described subject; lacks details |
| **Organization/ Paragraphs** | Details arranged in a clear order; strong beginning and ending | Details mostly arranged in order; good beginning and ending | Details not well connected; weak beginning and ending | No organization of details; lack of beginning or ending |
| **Voice** | Strong personality; clear connection between writer and subject | Writer involved; some connection between writer and subject | Writer lacking involvement; few feelings shown | Writer involvement, point of view missing |
| **Word Choice** | Specific, vivid language that appeals to several senses | Accurate, engaging language that appeals to one or two senses | Uninteresting language; little appeal to senses | Limited, vague language; repetitive |
| **Sentences** | Superior structure; excellent flow | Some varied beginnings; well constructed | Simple structures; little variety | Many errors; awkward; hard to read |
| **Conventions** | Excellent control; few or no errors | No serious errors to affect understanding | Weak control; enough errors to affect understanding | Many errors that prevent understanding |

Following are four models that respond to a prompt. Each model has been given a score, based on the rubric.

**Writing Prompt** Write a description of a pet. Use exact words to help readers see, hear, smell, and feel the pet's personality and appearance.

# Descriptive Writing Model *Score 4*

Some people think a fish makes a poor pet, but they never met my goldfish Mutt. He may not fetch or purr, but Mutt is beautiful, smart, and entertaining.

While most goldfish are solid orange-gold, Mutt looks as though an artist painted parts of him a velvety black. When he swims, his long fins and tail wave and shimmer. He is a silk kite with streamers.

I think Mutt is intelligent because he knows when it is time to eat. As soon as I get the food flakes, he glides close to me and points his mouth at the surface. He likes attention and comes close when I press my face to the glass. Then, at bedtime, he retires to his plastic "house."

Watching Mutt swim gracefully and slowly or dart like lightning around his aquarium keeps me entertained for hours. If I am tired or upset, Mutt gives me a calm, restful feeling.

**Focus/Ideas**   Strong, specific details that bring subject into focus

**Organization/Paragraphs**   Organized by traits, one per paragraph; strong beginning and ending

**Voice**   Clear communication of bond with pet; strong writer presence *(I press my face to the glass)*

**Word Choice**   Vivid verbs and modifiers that appeal to sight *(fetch, velvety, shimmer, gracefully, dart)*, hearing *(purr)*, and feeling *(calm, restful)*; metaphor *(a silk kite with streamers)*

**Sentences**   Interest through varied kinds and lengths of sentences; combined ideas

**Conventions**   No mechanical errors

## Descriptive Writing Model *Score 3*

My mom says our dog Rufus is Heinz 57 Variety. That means he isn't one breed but many breeds mixed together. Rufus is mixed up in more than one way. Yet he is so lovable I don't care.

Rufus barks when he wants out, which is a lot. As soon as he gets out, we here another bark. He is waiting to get in. Make up your mind, Rufus! He is supposed to be part chow.

He barks at anyone who comes to the door. Like he would bite their head off. Then they come in, and he wags his tail. And jumps up to lick them!

Mixed-up Rufus doesn't look exactly like any other dog. He has the head of a collie and the body of a German shepherd. His tail curls up and over like a chow's. When he looks at me with his big brown eyes, I think he looks like the best dog ever!

**Focus/Ideas**   All details focused on the subject of Rufus the dog; one sentence out of place *(He is…chow.)*

**Organization/Paragraphs**   Details in logical order with good connecting words

**Voice**   Writer's feelings for Rufus clear *(he is so lovable I don't care; the best dog ever)*

**Word Choice**   A few strong verbs and modifiers that appeal to sight *(wags, curls up and over, big brown)* and hearing *(barks)*

**Sentences**   Good variety of sentence kinds and lengths; some variety of sentence beginnings

**Conventions**   A spelling error *(here)*; two sentence fragments; lack of pronoun agreement *(anyone/their)*

## Descriptive Writing Model *Score 2*

> I don't have no pet and I would like one but mom and dad said we can't get one so I am writing about my neighbors cat Cheerio. She is orange and white and fat. I like how her tail curls over her back like a question mark. When you call her she sounds like she is saying me? The neighbor had two cats but one died which is sad. I buy treats for cheerio and taught her to sit up and roll over. which is a riet. she purrs like a rusty enjin.

**Focus/Ideas**   Focused on neighbor's cat; some descriptive details

**Organization/Paragraphs**   Little sense of organization; few connecting words; weak beginning; no end or paragraphs

**Voice**   Feelings shown (*I like how her tail, which is sad, a riet*)

**Word Choice**   Some details that appeal to sight and hearing; strong figurative language

**Sentences**   Some sentences strung together; one fragment; little variety; poor flow

**Conventions**   Errors in spelling (*riet, enjin*), punctuation (quotation marks, apostrophes, commas), verb tense, and capitalization; double negative (*don't have no*)

## Descriptive Writing Model *Score 1*

> George runs on a weel at night. George is mine gerbel I got him when I was sevin. He chews up tubes. he make a nest of the pieces. he is gray. George eats pellets and little pieces of fruit and carats. A bird eats seeds and fruit too I had a paraket. A gerbel is a kind of mouse. he sleeps a lot in the day. I put him in a fish tank but only a little bottle of water. he drink water out the tube. George has funny wiskers and black eyes.

**Focus/Ideas**   Details about birds distract from subject

**Organization/Paragraphs**   Details very disorganized; ideas not joined with connectors; no paragraphs; no ending

**Voice**   Writer's feeling for subject unclear

**Word Choice**   Mostly general words; some modifiers; some details appealing to sound and sight

**Sentences**   Overly simple constructions; run-ons

**Conventions**   Errors in spelling *(weel, gerbel, sevin, carats, paraket, wiskers),* capitalization, verb and pronoun usage, punctuation

# Persuasive Writing *Scoring Rubric*

| Score | 4 | 3 | 2 | 1 |
|---|---|---|---|---|
| **Focus/Ideas** | Excellent persuasive essay with clearly stated opinion and strong elaboration | Clear opinion supported by mostly persuasive reasons | Opinion not clearly stated; weak reasons or not enough reasons to support it | No stated opinion; details not focused on topic |
| **Organization/ Paragraphs** | Strong, convincing introduction; reasons presented in order of importance | Interesting introduction; reasons in order of importance | Weak or unclear introduction; reasons not clear or not in order of importance | No introduction; few reasons; order not logical |
| **Voice** | Concerned, committed writer behind words | Some sense of caring, concerned writer behind words | Little sense of writer involvement with essay | No sense of writer's personality or feelings evident |
| **Word Choice** | Effective use of persuasive words | Use of persuasive words adequate to good | Few persuasive words used in essay | No persuasive words used in essay |
| **Sentences** | Varied sentence structures; excellent flow and rhythm | Some varied sentence structures; few sentence errors | Sentence structures lacking variety; some sentence errors | Simple, choppy sentences; fragments and run-ons |
| **Conventions** | Excellent control of all mechanical aspects of writing | Few errors in grammar, spelling, punctuation, paragraphing | Some distracting mechanical errors | Many errors that prevent understanding |

Following are four models that respond to a prompt. Each model has been given a score, based on the rubric.

**Writing Prompt** What animal would be a good mascot for your school? State your choice and persuade your readers to accept it by giving several strong reasons why it is an excellent choice.

## Persuasive Writing Model *Score 4*

Go, Bulldogs, go! We should adopt the bulldog as our school mascot because there is so much to admire in a bulldog.

First, we say that the dog is people's best friend. A best friend is always there for you and supports you. Loyalty is part of a winning attitude for people too.

Second, like all dogs, bulldogs love people. A bulldog takes care of its family. For example, it would defend you from harm. Students at Benton Elementary are like a family, and a bulldog mascot would stand for the way we take care of each other.

Most important, a bulldog is strong and a great fighter. Once it grabs on, it doesn't let go. Don't we want to have that kind of staying power? If we play a game or meet a goal, we will give it our best and won't quit.

Now, don't you think Benton Bulldogs has a nice ring to it?

**Focus/Ideas** Opinion clearly stated; developed with good supporting reasons and details

**Organization/Paragraphs** Strong introduction; topic sentences give reasons in logical order; most important reason given last

**Voice** Writer's enthusiasm and personality evident

**Word Choice** Persuasive words with emotional appeal (*best friend, winning attitude, love, takes care of, family, staying power*)

**Sentences** Varied structures and kinds; connectors aid flow (*First, Second, For example, Most important, Now*)

**Conventions** No mechanical errors

## Persuasive Writing Model *Score 3*

I am voting for eagles to be our mascot for these reasons. One, eagles live around here. That is special. People drive from all over the state to watch them.

Also, eagles show pride in our country. They fly high and free. Thats why they are a symbol for the U.S. The name Eagles shows patriatizm and that we are a great school. Also, there are a lot of awesome pictures of eagles around so we could get a good picture for the school.

And eagles stand out from the rest. They can see far and fly so fast. They always get their prey. They are number one hunters. Don't we want to be the number one school?

You should vote for eagles as our school mascot.

**Focus/Ideas**  Clear opinion and good examples; some elaboration

**Organization/Paragraphs**  One reason to a paragraph; no order of importance apparent; connectors repetitive *(and, also)*

**Voice**  Writer's feelings stated; some sense of personality

**Word Choice**  Some persuasive words and phrases *(special, great school, number one)*; some dull words *(a lot of)*

**Sentences**  Some sentence variety; too many short, choppy sentences

**Conventions**  Error in spelling *(patriatizm)* and use of apostrophe *(thats* instead of *that's)*

# Persuasive Writing Model *Score 2*

Tigers are the coolest looking animal. I love to draw them. They have black stripes and sharp fangs. They stok very quiet through the jungle. Bam! There prey never knew what hit them.

Tigers are orange and black, and those are our school colors. See how that fits?

Another reason. Tigers be ferce, and they win in a fight. That's what we want our team to do.

Go Benton Tigers! Vote for tigers!

**Focus/Ideas**  Opinion not clearly stated at the beginning; irrelevant details weaken writer's argument *(I love to draw them, There prey never knew what hit them);* some good elaboration

**Organization/Paragraphs**  Introduction lacking; reasons in no apparent order

**Voice**  Writer's feelings clearly expressed

**Word Choice**  Few persuasive words; overuse of *are*

**Sentences**  Too many short, choppy sentences; lacks natural flow; sentence fragment

**Conventions**  Errors in spelling *(stok, there* instead of *their, ferce),* use of adverbs *(quiet* instead of *quietly)* and verbs *(be* instead of *are)*

## Persuasive Writing Model *Score 1*

> Shark would be good. Sharks have rows of real sharp teeth. It body is strong it swims and swims. And never sleeps. Sharks are different from fish. shark don't mess around they attack. they are eating mesheens. Did you ever see the movie <u>jaws</u>? a big shark eating people. you bewear of shark

**Focus/Ideas**   Opinion not clearly stated; information not presented as support for an argument

**Organization/Paragraphs**   No paragraphing or introduction; no organizational plan evident

**Voice**   Good sense of writer behind words

**Word Choice**   Vague, general words *(good, have, is, are);* needs more persuasive words

**Sentences**   Many fragments and run-ons; ideas incompletely communicated

**Conventions**   Errors in spelling *(mesheens, bewear)*, capitalization, end punctuation, usage *(real* instead of *really; shark* instead of *sharks),* subject-verb agreement *(shark don't* instead of *sharks don't);* pronouns *(It body* instead of *Its body)*

# Expository Writing *Scoring Rubric*

| Score | 4 | 3 | 2 | 1 |
|---|---|---|---|---|
| **Focus/Ideas** | Excellent explanation of process; steps explained clearly | Good explanation of process; steps mostly clear | Some focus on process; some steps missing or unclear | Explanation of process unfocused; steps missing |
| **Organization/ Paragraphs** | Clear introduction of topic; steps in order; appropriate connecting words | Adequate introduction of topic; most steps in correct order; some connecting words | Introduction weak; important steps missing or in wrong order; few connecting words | Introduction of topic missing; steps out of order; no connecting words |
| **Voice** | Engaging, straightforward, helpful | Somewhat engaging and helpful | Voice not always appropriate to subject matter | Voice lacking or inappropriate |
| **Word Choice** | Steps conveyed through specific, strong verbs and nouns | Steps outlined with clear nouns and verbs | Some vague, repetitive, or incorrect words | Clear nouns and verbs lacking; very limited word choices |
| **Sentences** | Well-crafted sentences; focus on imperative | Mostly imperative sentences; few sentence errors | Overly simple constructions; some errors | Many fragments; sense hard to follow |
| **Conventions** | Excellent control of all mechanical aspects of writing | Few mechanical errors | Some distracting mechanical errors | Many errors in mechanics that prevent understanding |

Following are four models that respond to a prompt. Each model has been given a score, based on the rubric.

**Writing Prompt** Write an expository essay explaining how to do or make something. For example, you could tell how to make pizza or put up a tent. List any materials needed. Use specific, strong verbs, and put the steps in order.

# Expository Writing Model *Score 4*

Everybody loves pizza, and this French bread pizza is quick and easy to make. First, get out the things you need: a sharp knife, a cookie sheet, a loaf of French bread, pizza sauce, shredded mozzarella cheese, and any other toppings you want.

Next, turn the oven on to 400°F. While it is heating up, carefully slice the bread in half the long way. Now spread pizza sauce to cover the top of the bread. Then cover the sauce with cheese. How much you use depends on how much you like cheese. Do not put on too much cheese, or some will fall off the bread and onto the cookie sheet.

Finally, add your favorite toppings, such as peppers, olives, sausage, or pepperoni. Place your pizza on the cookie sheet and bake it for 15 minutes. Let it cool for a few minutes and bite in!

**Focus/Ideas**   Clear main idea; all details explain the steps clearly

**Organization/Paragraphs**   Clear introduction; steps in order; helpful connectors (*First, Next, While, Now, Then, Finally*)

**Voice**   Warm and helpful, but serious about process

**Word Choice**   Precise nouns (*knife, cookie sheet, loaf, pizza sauce*) and specific verbs (*slice, spread, cover, bake*)

**Sentences**   Imperative sentences consistent with how-to format

**Conventions**   Excellent control; no mechanical errors

# Expository Writing Model *Score 3*

> To add beauty to your home, plant flowers around it. You will need a shovel, a spade, some potting soil, seedlings, and a watering can.
>
> First, you will getting the dirt reddy. Turn it over with a shovel. Crush any large chunks so the dirt is even and smooth.
>
> Now you can make holes for your seedlings with a spade. I make the hole big enough for the roots and a little deeper. Add a little potting soil at the bottom of the hole. Put the plant in. Hold it straight with one hand. Add potting soil with the other hand. Don't cover to much of the stem. Tamp down the dirt with you're palms.
>
> When you finnish planting the flowers, give them a good drink of water. This is because of the fact that the roots need a drink.

**Focus/Ideas**   Main idea clear, with most details focused on actions involved in process; last sentence wordy

**Organization/Paragraphs**   Introduces process and items needed; some use of connecting words; logical paragraph breaks

**Voice**   Writer pleasant *(To add beauty to your home)*; gives some helpful hints *(Hold it straight, Don't cover to much)*

**Word Choice**   Some strong verbs *(crush, tamp)*; some general words *(make, big, little, put, good)*

**Sentences**   Mostly imperative sentences; somewhat choppy style

**Conventions**   Errors in spelling *(reddy, to* instead of *too, you're* instead of *your, finnish)* and verb form *(getting* instead of *get)*

# Expository Writing Model *Score 2*

To get a raise in your allowance. This work for me. Be extra good the day your gonna ask. Like if your parents have to nag you to do stuff, do it before they can. Clean up the dinner table. do it before they ask you to. Act responsably. Like talk about how you need to be the boss of your own mony and savings and stuff. Look sad and tell how you have to spend all your mony on lunch and can't save any for important stuff like games or college. maybe do this two or three days.

**Focus/Ideas**   Main idea presented; details somewhat repetitive

**Organization/Paragraphs**   Weak introduction; no apparent organization; lack of connecting words; no paragraphs

**Voice**   Establishes personality; too informal (*gonna, like*)

**Word Choice**   Some general, vague words (*good, do, stuff*)

**Sentences**   Fragments and awkward sentences; mostly imperative sentences

**Conventions**   Errors in spelling (*your* instead of *you're, responsably, mony*), subject-verb agreement, capitalization, punctuation; incorrect verb form (*gonna*)

# Expository Writing Model *Score 1*

> I use matches some people use a flint. its a hard rock it makes sparks.
> Put big pieces on top but first twigs and paper. That burn easy. have you
> wood and twigs by you. Feed the fire. You can put pieces on each other.
> Like a tepee. Oh, wet or gren wood don't ketch fire. Smoky bear says be
> sure your fire is out. you mit dig around the fire pit

**Focus/Ideas**   Lacks main idea statement; includes irrelevant details

**Organization/Paragraphs**   No introduction of topic; details out of order; no connecting words; no paragraph breaks

**Voice**   No clear voice; delivery unsure and disorganized

**Word Choice**   Vague verbs (*put, have, is*)

**Sentences**   Many run-ons and fragments; extremely choppy; hard to follow

**Conventions**   Errors in spelling (*its* instead of *it's, gren, ketch, mit*), capitalization, punctuation, subject-verb agreement (*don't* instead of *doesn't*), pronoun usage (*you* instead of *your*)

# Evaluate Your Writing

You can evaluate your own writing by reading it over carefully. Think about what is good as well as what you can improve. As you read, ask yourself the following questions.

**How does my writing sound?**   Read it aloud to find out.

- If it sounds choppy, you might combine short sentences.
- Are there many sentences strung together with *and, because,* or *then?* "Unhook" a long stringy sentence by separating it into several sentences.
- Do most sentences begin with *I, the, it, she,* or *he?* Think of other ways to begin these sentences. Simply rearranging words might do the trick.
- Do ideas seem connected? If not, add transition words or phrases such as *finally* or *on the other hand.* These words connect ideas and help your sentences flow.

**Is the style appropriate?**   Who is your audience? (friends, your principal, a newspaper editor) What is your purpose? (to inform, to persuade, to entertain) Sentence fragments, informal language, and slang may be appropriate for e-mails or quick notes among friends. A more formal style suits written assignments.

**Does your writing address the assignment?**

- Look for key words in the writing prompt. For example:

  <u>Compare and contrast</u> a <u>bike</u> and a <u>car</u>.
  Tell <u>two similarities and two differences</u>.

  *Topic: bike and car*

  *What you need to do: Compare and contrast*

  *What to include: Two similarities and two differences*

- Other kinds of key words in writing prompts include *describe, explain, summarize, examples, why,* and *how.*

**Is your writing focused?** Are all the sentences about the main idea? Take out or refocus sentences that wander off into unimportant details.

**Is there enough elaboration and support?** Your writing may be unclear if you don't elaborate on your ideas. Supply information that readers need to know.

- Use sensory details to make your writing seem fresh and to give readers pictures, but avoid sounding flowery.
- If you give an opinion, supply strong supporting reasons.
- Expand on a main idea with several telling details.
- When necessary, define a term or give examples.

**Is your beginning strong?** Does a question, a surprising fact, or an amusing detail capture a reader's interest?

**Is your ending satisfying?** A conclusion may restate the main idea in a new way, tell what you feel or what you have learned, or pose a question to readers to think about. Whatever it does, it should signal that you have finished.

**Have you used effective words—and not too many of them?** Have you chosen your words carefully?

- Strong verbs, precise nouns, and vivid adjectives make your writing clear and lively.
- Are there awkward phrases you can replace with a word or two? For example, replace *due to the fact that* with *because* and *at this point in time* with *now*.

## Checklist

☐ My writing sounds smooth and easy to read.

☐ I have used an appropriate style for my audience and purpose.

☐ My writing addresses the prompt or assignment.

☐ My writing is focused.

☐ I have used enough elaboration and support.

☐ I have a strong beginning.

☐ I have a satisfying conclusion.

☐ I have used effective words and avoided wordiness.

# Grammar and Writing Lessons

## LESSON 1

# Sentences

- A **declarative sentence,** or statement, tells something. It ends with a period.
  Specially trained dogs help people with disabilities.
- An **interrogative sentence** asks a question. It ends with a question mark.
  What kinds of jobs can these dogs do?
- An **imperative sentence** gives a command or makes a request. It ends with a period. *You* is the understood subject.
  Read this newspaper article about some heroic canines.
- An **exclamatory sentence** shows strong feeling. It ends with an exclamation mark.
  How interesting this article is! That dog is amazing!
- An **interjection** is a word or a group of words that expresses strong feeling. It is not a complete sentence.
  Oh, my! Wow! Ouch! Hooray!

**A** Write *D* if the sentence is declarative. Write *IN* if it is interrogative. Write *IM* if it is imperative. Write *E* if it is exclamatory.

1. Where did you find your new puppy?
2. The animal shelter rescues abandoned pets.
3. What a wonderful job that place does!
4. Visit the shelter in your neighborhood.
5. You will be amazed at the variety of animals.
6. Do they have snakes and lizards at the shelter?
7. Call this number for that information.
8. Wow! A pet snake would be terrific!

**B** Write each sentence, adding capitalization and the correct end mark. Then write *D* if the sentence is declarative, *IM* if it is imperative, *IN* if it is interrogative, or *E* if it is exclamatory.

1. a dog is fiercely loyal to its owner
2. what a great watchdog Wilbur is
3. is Wilbur a German shepherd
4. we adopted Wilbur as a pup
5. watch him do his tricks
6. have you ever heard a dog sing
7. wilbur howls while I practice piano
8. that is an unbelievable racket
9. why does Wilbur bark when someone comes to the door
10. he is defending his territory and his family

**C** Complete each sentence with words from the box. Write the sentences using capitalization and correct end marks.

| | |
|---|---|
| to their owners' illnesses | that is |
| about cancer-sniffing dogs | read more about this |
| have defended their owners | cancer in people |

11. many dogs
12. are dogs sensitive
13. read this article
14. these dogs can sense
15. what an amazing life-saving act
16. where can I

# Test Preparation

Read the paragraph. Write the letter of the word that identifies each kind of sentence.

(1) The bond between pets and owners is strong. (2) How many pets do you know? (3) Do they sleep with their owners? (4) Some pets and owners are inseparable. (5) Can pets and owners really look alike? (6) That can happen with time. (7) That's incredible! (8) Your pet depends on you. (9) Give it food, water, love, and exercise. (10) A healthy, loving pet is a part of the family.

1   **A**   declarative
  **B**   interrogative
  **C**   imperative
  **D**   exclamatory

2. **A**   declarative
  **B**   interrogative
  **C**   imperative
  **D**   exclamatory

3. **A**   declarative
  **B**   interrogative
  **C**   imperative
  **D**   exclamatory

4. **A**   declarative
  **B**   interrogative
  **C**   imperative
  **D**   exclamatory

5. **A**   declarative
  **B**   interrogative
  **C**   imperative
  **D**   exclamatory

6. **A**   declarative
  **B**   interrogative
  **C**   imperative
  **D**   exclamatory

7. **A**   declarative
  **B**   interrogative
  **C**   imperative
  **D**   exclamatory

8. **A**   declarative
  **B**   interrogative
  **C**   imperative
  **D**   exclamatory

9. **A**   declarative
  **B**   interrogative
  **C**   imperative
  **D**   exclamatory

10. **A**   declarative
  **B**   interrogative
  **C**   imperative
  **D**   exclamatory

# Review

Write the mark that should end each sentence. Then write *D* if the sentence is declarative, *IN* if it is interrogative, *IM* if it is imperative, and *E* if it is exclamatory.

1. Some cartoons are based on pets and owners
2. Do you like the comic strip Garfield
3. What a great cartoon that is
4. Garfield the cat "owns" his human Jon Arbuckle
5. Isn't Odie the name of Jon's dog
6. Why does Garfield pick on Odie all the time
7. Please be careful, Odie
8. Don't let Garfield trick you again
9. Garfield is such a rascal
10. He has a soft spot for his teddy bear, Pookie

Write each sentence. Make any necessary corrections in capitalization and punctuation.

11. does your pet understand what you say
12. my cat, Ragamuffin, communicates with me
13. hey! You forgot my food
14. she butts my leg with her head
15. a loud purr means she is happy
16. how does a cat purr
17. scratch my head right here
18. what a wonderful human you are
19. ragamuffin talks with her voice, tail, and claws
20. give your pet plenty of love and attention
21. who needs words anyway
22. watch Ragamuffin get what she wants

# Show, Don't Tell

When you write about yourself, **show**, **don't tell**, how you feel.

**Tell**     I was nervous.

**Show**   My voice squeaked and my knees knocked.

 Use words from the word bank or your own words to replace the words in ( ). Write the sentences. Write a final sentence that shows feelings.

| | |
|---|---|
| jumped in circles and yapped | like a ball of red fur with feet |
| giggled wildly and zoomed | romping and playing with his new friend |

1. My little brother Jason (was excited and went ) into the kitchen. Dad was bringing home our new dog!
2. The puppy looked (cute).
3. We named her Sparky because she (was so energetic).
4. Jason looked forward to (spending time with her).
5. ____

 Write a paragraph describing a pet you have known. Use vivid details and images to show (not tell) how the pet and you feel. If you wish, use the questions below to help you.

What kind of pet was it, and what was its main personality trait?

What did it look like?

When did you first see it?

What did you do together?

How did you feel about each other?

# Memoir

A **memoir** tells a story from the author's life. Vivid descriptions draw the reader into the author's personal "world." Words such as *I, me,* and *mine* show that the narrator sees things from a personal point of view.

*I, my,* and *me* show a personal point of view.

Strong word choice sets the scene.

Different kinds of sentences and an intentional fragment keep the story interesting.

### A Childhood Memory

I remember my tenth birthday as if it were yesterday.

I ran home from school through almost a foot of squishy snow. At the corner of Oak and Lavey, I skidded on a patch of ice and crashed into a snowbank. Now my mittens were soaked and my boots were leaky.

Finally, I made it! Home at last! I streaked up the steep front steps, unlocked the front door (with all three keys), and burst into the living room. What great birthday surprise had Mom and Aunt Susu planned for me this time?

# Subjects and Predicates

A sentence must have a subject and a predicate. The **subject** tells whom or what the sentence is about. All the words in the subject are the **complete subject**. The most important word in the complete subject is the **simple subject**. It may be more than one word, such as *Mrs. Williams*.

> My favorite neighbor lives in a big, yellow house.

> The simple subject is *neighbor.*

The **predicate** tells what the subject is or does. All the words in the predicate are the **complete predicate**. The most important word in the predicate is the **simple predicate**, or the verb. It may have more than one word, such as *has lived*.

> My favorite neighbor lives in a big yellow house.

> The simple predicate is *lives.*

A **fragment** is a group of words that lacks a subject or a predicate. The fragment below lacks a subject.

> Lived in her house for 60 years.

A **run-on** is two or more complete sentences run together.

> Mrs. Moy has a flower garden her roses are beautiful.

> I'm not a gardener, everything I touch wilts.

**A** Write each sentence. Divide the complete subject and complete predicate with a line. Underline the simple subject once and the simple predicate twice.

1. Her house is surrounded by a white picket fence.
2. Many beautiful flowers grow in the front yard.
3. Mrs. Williams works in her gardens every sunny day.
4. Two huge oak trees tower over her house.

**B** Write *F* for a fragment. Write *RO* for a run-on. Write *S* for a complete sentence.

1. Visits the nursing home on Oak Street once a month.
2. The children bring pictures and vases as gifts.
3. The leader of Troop 133.
4. Mr. Clay plays piano sometimes he brings his dogs.
5. The residents love to pet Lefty and Bear.
6. Cheers up many of the elderly people.
7. Music soothes and stimulates people of all ages.
8. Animal companions also bring new life to the home.
9. The scouts feel good about themselves, the residents enjoy talking to young people.
10. A win-win situation for all.

**C** Add your own words to each of the following fragments to make a complete sentence. Write the new sentence. Underline the simple subject and circle the simple predicate.

11. My great-grandmother
12. was her name
13. This red-haired teenager
14. Family friends on the East Side
15. hired as a governess for the children of a wealthy family
16. married Thomas O'Brien, an auto mechanic
17. Wedding pictures of Thomas and Molly
18. had twelve children
19. Their twelfth child
20. was my grandmother and my namesake

# Test Preparation

Write the letter of the phrase that correctly identifies the underlined part of the sentence.

1. <u>Our local police officers</u> meet many community needs.
   - **A** complete subject
   - **B** complete predicate
   - **C** simple subject
   - **D** simple predicate

2. They <u>patrol</u> the streets.
   - **A** complete subject
   - **B** complete predicate
   - **C** simple subject
   - **D** simple predicate

3. Of course, trained <u>detectives</u> investigate crimes.
   - **A** complete subject
   - **B** complete predicate
   - **C** simple subject
   - **D** simple predicate

4. Police <u>regulate traffic flow at an accident scene</u>.
   - **A** complete subject
   - **B** complete predicate
   - **C** simple subject
   - **D** simple predicate

5. Officers <u>may give</u> tickets to drivers.
   - **A** complete subject
   - **B** complete predicate
   - **C** simple subject
   - **D** simple predicate

6. <u>Their goal</u> is to make the streets safe.
   - **A** complete subject
   - **B** complete predicate
   - **C** simple subject
   - **D** simple predicate

7. <u>Citizens</u> in trouble can call the police for help.
   - **A** complete subject
   - **B** complete predicate
   - **C** simple subject
   - **D** simple predicate

8. Many TV shows <u>have depicted the lives of police officers</u>.
   - **A** complete subject
   - **B** complete predicate
   - **C** simple subject
   - **D** simple predicate

9. <u>Most of these shows</u> make police work seem exciting.
   - **A** complete subject
   - **B** complete predicate
   - **C** simple subject
   - **D** simple predicate

10. In fact, much of the work <u>is</u> routine.
    - **A** complete subject
    - **B** complete predicate
    - **C** simple subject
    - **D** simple predicate

# Review

✓ Write each sentence. Divide the complete subject and complete predicate with a line.

1. City neighborhoods offer interesting histories.
2. Each neighborhood reflects a distinct heritage.
3. Many immigrants from a particular country settled together in one location.
4. Their common culture gave them a feeling of belonging.
5. Polish, Italian, and Chinese neighborhoods formed early in our city's history.

✓ Write *F* for a fragment. Write *RO* for a run-on. Write *S* for a complete sentence.

6. Most of the people in our urban neighborhood.
7. We celebrate Mexico's Independence Day, everyone enjoys the big parade.
8. Many people speak Spanish.
9. Love eating at the many great Mexican restaurants.
10. My favorite dish is chiles rellenos these are deep-fried chiles stuffed with cheese.

✓ Write the simple subject and the simple predicate in each sentence.

11. More and more people live in subdivisions today.
12. Large houses stand side by side in rows.
13. In a subdivision, you seldom know many neighbors.
14. People in your neighborhood will come from all walks of life.
15. They may represent many different cultures.
16. Busy lives isolate people from one another.
17. A block party can bring neighbors together.
18. Neighbors share food and fun together.

# Tone

> A writer's **tone** expresses his or her attitude toward the subject. Word choice, sentence structure, and word pictures made by details and comparisons create the tone in a piece of writing.

Write the word from the box that describes the tone of each paragraph.

| |
|---|
| humorous    spooky    serious |

1. Wednesday is garbage day. Every Tuesday I have to separate all of the recycling into different bags: one for plastic, one for glass, and one for paper. All of the paper has to be clean and flat, and all of the glass has to be washed and dried.

2. The night was still. We could hear an owl hooting softly in the distance. Who-o-o. . . who-o-o. . . . As we crept slowly around Maynard's barn, every crunching leaf made us jump.

3. "Hold it!" Mom stopped me at the foot of the stairs. She had that look in her eye. I know that look. It's the look of doom! She pointed silently at my feet. What? What's the problem? I looked slowly down at my feet and saw the potential disaster. My socks! One was orange and one was white. "Thanks, Mom," I muttered as I trudged back up the stairs.

Write a paragraph about something that has happened to you. Use a serious, spooky, or humorous tone.

# Character Sketch

A **character sketch** makes a person or story character come alive for the reader. It vividly describes the person's actions and character traits.

Topic sentence "sets up" three character traits.

Detail sentences tell actions for each trait.

Conclusion tells writer's feelings about the character.

**The Gift of Mother Fletcher**

Mother Fletcher in *Mother Fletcher's Gift* is a mysterious woman, but she is also kind and funny.

She doesn't reveal her real first name or just how old she is. At first, Officer O'Brien doesn't know what to make of her because she gives strange answers to his questions.

Later, when O'Brien thinks he has finally finished with her, Mother Fletcher gives him sweaters that she knitted for him and his wife. When he stops by to thank her, she invites the O'Briens to Christmas dinner.

As we learn at the end of the story, Mother Fletcher has a great sense of humor. She tells funny stories to O'Brien's daughter about how she knew Santa Claus when he was a little boy. She tells Officer O'Brien that her age is "full-grown."

Mother Fletcher's real gift is that she can teach us all how to feel young, even when we get old!

# Independent and Dependent Clauses

An **independent clause** has a subject and verb and can stand alone as a complete sentence. A **dependent clause** has a subject and a verb but cannot stand alone as a complete sentence. It is introduced by a conjunction such as *before, if, since,* or *although.* A complex sentence contains an independent and a dependent clause.

In the following complex sentences, the independent clause is underlined once; the dependent clause is underlined twice. The dependent clause is followed by a comma when it comes before the independent clause.

Lucinda's relatives were in a makeshift boat before they reached America.

Before they reached America, Lucinda's relatives were in a makeshift boat.

**A** Write *I* if the group of words is an independent clause. Write *D* if it is a dependent clause and circle the conjunction.

1. Before the U.S. Coast Guard cutter towed them.
2. The perilous journey lasted two days.
3. Lucinda's family moved to West New York, New Jersey.
4. If the dog has not been found.
5. Whenever she heard a Spanish song.
6. Since she lived in an apartment building.
7. Some homes had cement lawns and paved driveways.
8. It was all too confusing.
9. Although he didn't feel like it.
10. Many people didn't know one another.

**B** Write each sentence. Underline the independent clause once and the dependent clause twice.

1. When you move, it can be hard to make friends.
2. The task is harder still if you speak a different language.
3. Before the first day of school arrived, I worried.
4. The new home would not feel like home until I made friends.
5. Although I have many friends now, once I had none.
6. I found a good friend after I joined the band.
7. Julio, Denise, and Martina have been my friends since I started third grade.
8. I can speak English well although my parents still struggle.
9. Because I am shy, I must make myself talk to new people.
10. When you meet new people, smile and ask them about themselves.

**C** Add an independent clause to each dependent clause to make a complex sentence. Write the sentences. Use correct punctuation and capitalization.

11. _____ because she wants to be a writer
12. after Anna heard about the story-writing contest _____
13. _____ until her fingers became cramped
14. _____ where she can find synonyms for words
15. since I am a decent artist _____
16. when she had finished writing _____
17. if she asks my opinion _____
18. _____ because I love to draw ghosts and other spooky things
19. _____ before she makes up her mind
20. if she really likes the pictures _____

# Test Preparation

Write the letter of the phrase that best identifies the underlined words in each sentence.

1. <u>When I heard something in the bushes</u>, I was scared at first.

   A  independent clause
   B  subject
   C  dependent clause
   D  none of the above

2. <u>A dirty, skinny little dog crept out</u> when I called.

   A  independent clause
   B  fragment
   C  dependent clause
   D  none of the above

3. I thought it was lost <u>because</u> it had a collar.

   A  independent clause
   B  conjunction
   C  dependent clause
   D  none of the above

4. When I looked <u>at the collar</u>, I learned the dog's name.

   A  independent clause
   B  conjunction
   C  dependent clause
   D  none of the above

5. Lucky came <u>when</u> I called.

   A  independent clause
   B  conjunction
   C  dependent clause
   D  none of the above

6. If the phone number on the collar was correct, <u>I could call the owners</u>.

   A  independent clause
   B  subject
   C  dependent clause
   D  none of the above

7. I gave Lucky food and a bath <u>before I called them</u>.

   A  independent clause
   B  predicate
   C  dependent clause
   D  none of the above

8. After they <u>heard the good news</u>, the Smiths were happy.

   A  independent clause
   B  run-on
   C  dependent clause
   D  none of the above

# Review

Write *I* for each independent clause. Write *D* for each dependent clause.

1. parents want the best for their children
2. they insist on a good education
3. because it prepares young people for the future
4. if you lack the skills for a certain job
5. you may need classes in that area
6. when you get a college degree
7. many areas and occupations open up to you
8. although I am a good student
9. my parents still nag me about studying hard
10. since I started school

Write the letter of the independent clause that can be matched with each dependent clause.

11. If a friend asks for my help,
12. When Joe lost his jacket,
13. Although we didn't find it,
14. Because I had an extra jacket,
15. Where friendship is concerned,

A  I helped him look for it.
B  he appreciated my help.
C  I always help.
D  kindness is the best plan.
E  I loaned it to Joe.

Write each sentence. Underline the independent clause once and the dependent clause twice. Circle the conjunction.

16. Because both my parents work, I help out at home.
17. I start supper when they will be late.
18. I usually make spaghetti since that is my specialty.
19. My brother sets the table while I cook the noodles.
20. Although he complains, he really likes doing it.

**WRITER'S CRAFT**

# Voice

> **Voice** shows a writer's personality through tone and word choice. It reveals feelings and makes one person's writing sound different from everyone else's. Writers should use a voice that suits their subject.

 Write the letter of the word that best describes the voice of each writer.

| **A** Serious | **B** Friendly | **C** Sarcastic |
|---|---|---|

1. The police responded quickly to the woman's call.
2. You'll never guess what my dog's name is!
3. Electric earmuffs! Just what every girl wants.
4. The party begins at noon, and everyone's invited.
5. New Jersey is located on the Atlantic Ocean.
6. Those greasy fries are so good for us all!
7. Could you turn that music up louder, so we'll all be deaf?
8. Many lost pets end up in an animal shelter.
9. Would you like me to show you around the place?
10. Volunteers each work four hours a week.

 Follow each set of directions to write a sentence with a distinctive voice.

11. Write a sentence about a lost pet using a serious voice.
12. Write a sentence about a special event using a friendly voice.
13. Write a sentence about a weird gift using a sarcastic voice.
14. Write a sentence about a food using a serious voice.
15. Write a sentence about a book using a friendly voice.

# Journal Entry

A **journal entry** tells about "a day in the life" of the writer. A good journal entry includes memorable events and details.

**First Day of School!**

**September 7**

Voice is honest and straightforward.

It was chillier than usual this morning when I woke up. I was anxious to see what my new classmates would be like. My new pants and dark green sweater and my backpack crammed full of supplies were sitting in the chair in my room. I was ready for my first day of middle school.

Writer includes description and opinions.

After breakfast (just cereal), I hurried up to Central Street to wait for the bus. I'm going to take a city bus to school from now on, and it costs seventy-five cents each way. Already I can see that sixth grade is more expensive than fifth.

Writer uses interesting details.

There were many students that I didn't know in my homeroom. I plopped down next to a boy named Mario who speaks English and Spanish. I think we'll be friends because we both play chess. Maybe we'll join the chess club. It looks as if this might be a good year.

# Compound and Complex Sentences

A **simple sentence** has a complete subject and a complete predicate.

The rain forest is being destroyed.

A **compound sentence** has two or more simple sentences joined by a comma and a conjunction such as *and, but,* or *or.*

The rain forest is being destroyed, and many of its plants and animals are disappearing.

A **complex sentence** has one independent clause and one or more dependent clauses introduced by a conjunction such as *if, because, after,* or *since.*

The rain forest is being destroyed because people cut down too many trees.

A **compound-complex sentence** has more than one independent clause and at least one dependent clause.

Because people cut down too many trees, the rain forest is being destroyed, and many of its plants and animals are disappearing.

Ⓐ Write *simple, compound, complex,* or *compound-complex* to identify each sentence.

1. Because they have leaves year-round, tropical rain forest trees are evergreen trees.
2. The trees grow tall and close together.
3. The forest ranger warned the hikers, but they did not listen.
4. After the rain ended, animals hunted and birds sang.
5. Whenever she can, Paula wakes before sunrise.
6. Do you like hot, humid weather?

**B** Write each sentence. Underline the conjunction that joins the two clauses. Write *CD* if the sentence is a compound sentence. Write *CX* if it is a complex sentence.

1. Trees take water in through their roots, and then they pump it upward throughout the system.
2. A tree is a living organism, but it looks dead in the winter.
3. Since many trees lose their leaves in winter, they stand bare through the cold months.
4. We must replace trees, or the world will become a barren place.
5. When people cut down trees, they often do not think about the consequences.

**C** Join each pair of simple sentences with the conjunction in ( ). Write the compound or complex sentence. Change punctuation and capital letters as necessary.

6. ___ Trees give off oxygen.
   They are essential to life on Earth. (because)
7. A tropical forest seems lush. ___
   Its soil is actually thin and poor. (but)
8. ___ People cut down the rain forest trees.
   The soil is soon swept away by heavy rains. (when)
9. This practice must be stopped. ___
   We will be left with deserts in place of lush forests. (or)
10. ___ The forests are allowed to disappear.
    We will lose many irreplaceable organisms. (if)

# Test Preparation

✓ Write the letter of the phrase that identifies each sentence.

**1.** Many plants provide food, but we have not discovered most of them yet.

   **A** simple sentence
   **B** compound sentence
   **C** complex sentence
   **D** compound-complex sentence

**2.** If we ate a more varied diet, we would be healthier.

   **A** simple sentence
   **B** compound sentence
   **C** complex sentence
   **D** compound-complex sentence

**3.** People get into a dietary rut, and they eat the same foods.

   **A** simple sentence
   **B** compound sentence
   **C** complex sentence
   **D** compound-complex sentence

**4.** When he was lost in the forest, he looked for food, but he didn't find any.

   **A** simple sentence
   **B** compound sentence
   **C** complex sentence
   **D** compound-complex sentence

**5.** The heavy rain had soaked everything in camp.

   **A** simple sentence
   **B** compound sentence
   **C** complex sentence
   **D** compound-complex sentence

**6.** The explorers picked up their packs, and the journey continued.

   **A** simple sentence
   **B** compound sentence
   **C** complex sentence
   **D** compound-complex sentence

**7.** Although they wore insect repellent, they were badly bitten.

   **A** simple sentence
   **B** compound sentence
   **C** complex sentence
   **D** compound-complex sentence

**8.** They had discovered fifty new species of plants and animals.

   **A** simple sentence
   **B** compound sentence
   **C** complex sentence
   **D** compound-complex sentence

# Review

 Write *simple, compound, complex,* or *compound-complex* to identify each sentence.

1. A gorilla watched us closely, but he made no move.
2. Until he left, no one moved, and all the hikers held their breath.
3. When I heard noises in the brush, I expected a lion.
4. Since few cats are left in this forest, a sighting was unlikely.
5. After breakfast we hiked ten miles to the waterhole.
6. Bill got a blister, and Angela ran out of water.
7. When we got there, we saw hippos, and everyone took photos.
8. Our expedition was exhausting, but it was exciting.

Write each sentence. Underline the conjunction that joins the two clauses. Write *CD* if the sentence is a compound sentence. Write *CX* if it is a complex sentence.

9. Tropical and temperate rain forests have evergreen trees, but trees of the cloud rain forests drop their leaves.
10. The regions around the equator are hot year round, and they receive huge amounts of rain.
11. If we don't stop the destruction of the rain forests, this precious resource will be lost.
12. Because ivory is in great demand, elephants are killed illegally.
13. It is illegal to hunt elephants, but poachers do not respect laws.
14. When its population becomes too small, a species cannot reproduce successfully.
15. Then it becomes extinct, or it exists only in zoos.

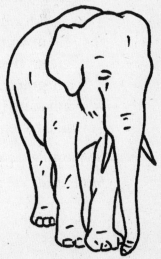

# Supporting Your Ideas

When you write, **supporting your ideas** helps you "make your case." Facts and details that support the main idea help convince readers that your argument is valid.

 In each paragraph, one sentence does not support the main idea. Write this sentence.

1. *Main Idea:* We need to protect our wildlife.

    Many kinds of animals are in danger of disappearing altogether. Deforestation and pollution threaten many species. My favorite animal is the bald eagle. The world would not be as nice a place if animals become extinct.

2. *Main Idea:* I need a new pair of gym shoes.

    I have three pairs of shoes. I got my gym shoes two years ago and they're getting too small. The soles are wearing out, and my toes are in danger of showing through! Most important, I could skid on my worn soles and injure myself.

3. *Main Idea:* Thomas Edison was a great inventor.

    Edison invented the light bulb, which lets us read anytime. He invented the phonograph and motion pictures, which make great entertainment. He also invented devices that made the telegraph and the telephone more practical and useful. This amazing inventor held patents on 1,000 inventions! I would like to read more about Thomas Edison.

 Write four sentences that support the following main idea:
*Main Idea:* We should clean up our parks.

# Problem/Solution

A convincing **problem/solution** essay makes a strong case by using supporting facts and details. Make your sentences clear and direct.

## Give Us a Bump!

First sentence states a problem that the essay addresses.

Cars speed down La Cienega Street. This is especially dangerous because kids often play there. Something needs to be done!

Each topic sentence in paragraphs 3, 4, and 5 is supported with details.

La Cienega is a busy street where many kids play. There are no stop signs or speed bumps to slow cars down. Sometimes cars whiz by at 40 miles per hour! How can they do that on a neighborhood street where kids play ball and ride bikes? When a car zooms by, kids dash out of the way.

Speeding cars are often noisy too. There is an old black Chevy with a loud muffler. This car roars by many nights around 6 and invades our "peaceful" dinner hour.

A speeding car could hit the parked cars. People who park on the street shouldn't have to worry about their cars' safety. My mom is afraid that our car might get hit and our insurance will increase.

Last paragraph gives a solution to the problem and supporting details.

For all these reasons, I think the city should put a speed bump on our block. This would make drivers slow down. It would make our neighborhood a safer, quieter place.

# Common and Proper Nouns

A **common noun** names any person, place, or thing. Common nouns are not capitalized.

> The <u>feathers</u> floated above the <u>boy</u> in the <u>pool</u>.

A **proper noun** names a particular person, place, or thing. Capitalize the first word and each important word of a proper noun.

> <u>Uncle Tim</u> recited the <u>Pledge of Allegiance</u> in <u>Hob Park</u>.

Capitalize days, months, and holidays. Capitalize the first word and all important words in a title.

> <u>Memorial Day</u> is on the last <u>Monday</u> in <u>May</u>.

> Please return the book *The Adventures of Hercules*.

Abbreviated proper nouns appear in addresses, titles and initials in names, and names of days, months, and states. These abbreviations begin with capital letters. Many end with periods.

> Contact <u>Rev.</u> Samuel <u>B.</u> Farb, <u>Jr.,</u> at 1556 Heather <u>St.</u>, Syracuse, <u>NY</u> 13210 before <u>Tues.</u>, <u>Jan.</u> 31.

 Rewrite each sentence using correct capitalization.

1. mr. klein moved to tulsa, oklahoma, on wed., dec. 14.
2. The choir sang "america the beautiful" on the fourth of july.
3. The plant palace on thomas road is open tuesday to saturday.
4. We will visit the statue of liberty in june.
5. I addressed the letter to sen. s. leoni at 356 sherwood dr., beloit, wi 53511.

**B** Write *P* if the list shows proper nouns. Write *C* if the list shows common nouns. Then add another example to each list.

1. poodle, collie, terrier
2. Idaho, Kansas, Alabama
3. Missouri River, Lake Superior, Gulf of Mexico
4. roses, daffodils, daisies
5. King Blvd., Ashton St., Twelfth Ave.
6. Disney World, Universal Studios, Knotts Berry Farm
7. Sunday, Tuesday, Friday
8. Ms., Maj., Rep.
9. minutes, hours, days
10. loafers, sneakers, sandals

**C** Write each sentence. Capitalize the proper nouns.

11. Our pets include a dog named cinnamon, a cat named sir nibs, and a cockatoo named pretty boy.
12. It was hard moving them from providence, rhode island, to des moines, iowa.
13. The best pet store in town is george's pet emporium on south seventh street.
14. The office of dr. barnes is located on highway 38 one mile south of town.
15. Have you visited the corn palace in mitchell, south dakota?
16. Let's meet in huber park on saturday, march 26, to fly our kites.
17. My favorite authors are mark twain, j. k. rowling, and bill bryson.
18. On thanksgiving day I read my younger brother jake a book called *a turkey comes to dinner.*
19. We visited yellowstone national park and the grand canyon.
20. The author of *a cat named soccer* grew up in chicago near wrigley field.

# Test Preparation

Write the letter of the answer that is correctly capitalized.

1.  **A** president Abraham lincoln
    **B** president Abraham Lincoln
    **C** President Abraham Lincoln
    **D** President abraham Lincoln

2.  **A** 1735 west garden Way
    **B** 1735 West Garden Way
    **C** 1735 West Garden way
    **D** 1735 west garden way

3.  **A** the book *A Wrinkle in Time*
    **B** the book *a Wrinkle in Time*
    **C** the book *A wrinkle in time*
    **D** the book *A Wrinkle In Time*

4.  **A** American youth soccer organization
    **B** American Youth soccer organization
    **C** American Youth Soccer organization
    **D** American Youth Soccer Organization

5.  **A** Gen. Ulysses s. Grant
    **B** Gen. Ulysses S. Grant
    **C** gen. Ulysses s. Grant
    **D** Gen. Ulysses S. grant

6.  **A** Wednesday, February 12
    **B** wednesday, February 12
    **C** Wednesday, february 12
    **D** wednesday, february 12

7.  **A** hopkinsville, KY 42240
    **B** hopkinsville, Ky 42240
    **C** Hopkinsville, ky 42240
    **D** Hopkinsville, KY 42240

8.  **A** the song "turkey in the straw"
    **B** the song "Turkey in The Straw"
    **C** the song "Turkey in the Straw"
    **D** the song "Turkey In The Straw"

9.  **A** a parade on Memorial Day
    **B** a Parade on Memorial day
    **C** a parade on memorial day
    **D** a Parade on Memorial Day

10. **A** a statue in Central park
    **B** a Statue in Central Park
    **C** a statue in Central Park
    **D** a statue in central park

# Review

Write *P* if the underlined noun is a proper noun. Write *C* if it is a common noun.

1. Mr. Williams teaches <u>biology</u>.
2. He feeds birds seeds and suet in <u>winter</u>.
3. <u>Gabe Trotter</u> writes a column about nature.
4. Visit <u>Nehring Forest Preserve</u> to observe wildlife.
5. Dr. Keith Herbert teaches zoology at the <u>university</u>.
6. The zoo in <u>Brookfield</u> is quite large.
7. In the <u>West</u>, you can see wild horses and buffalo.
8. The San Diego Zoo has pandas from <u>China</u>.

Write *correct* if the group of words is capitalized correctly. If it has an error in capitalization, rewrite it correctly.

9. independence Day picnic
10. the movie *Home for the Holidays*
11. the Greatest Day of my Life
12. my best friend Oscar z. Gonzales

Write each sentence. Correct any errors in capitalization.

13. The Monarch butterflies migrate from the United States to mexico.
14. Many Scientists study the migration patterns of animals.
15. Some birds fly from north America to south America and back.
16. *The tarantula in my purse* is a nonfiction book by jean Craighead george.
17. Please send the magazine *national geographic* to this new address: 9138 east Lincoln hwy., Jonesboro, Ar 72401.
18. Han, wes, and aaron will go to camp wachaweechee with their Scout Troop in july.

# Good Beginnings

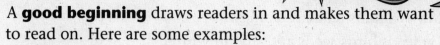

A **good beginning** draws readers in and makes them want to read on. Here are some examples:

| | |
|---|---|
| **Excitement** | Bang! Zoom! The go-cart screamed down the hill. |
| **Curiosity** | Wendy had no idea what was around the corner. |
| **Mood** | Was that the wind howling or a human scream? |

 Read each pair of beginnings. Write the letter of the better beginning.

**1. A** "Where in the world are my gloves?" yelled the captain.

   **B** The captain couldn't find his gloves.

**2. A** There was no noise.

   **B** It was quiet—almost too quiet.

**3. A** My cat is funny.

   **B** I never thought cats could speak.

**4. A** I couldn't just leave that poor baby bird alone on the ground.

   **B** Sometimes animals need our help.

**5. A** This paragraph is about air pollution and how we can avoid it.

   **B** Imagine having to wear a mask every day!

**6. A** Mr. Grimps was not happy.

   **B** Mr. Grimps chased the terrified kids around the block.

 Write two possible good beginnings for this paragraph.

_____. After that, I was no longer allowed to go into the stables without a grown-up. But I still rode every day. Appleton was still my favorite horse because he had a great sense of humor. And after a while, we became friends. We forgot all about the day he knocked me over!

# Writing for Tests

Think about <u>something interesting that happened to you</u> involving a <u>pet or a friend</u>. It might have been happy, like bringing home a new kitten, or sad, like saying goodbye to a good friend. Write a <u>narrative</u> showing what happened and <u>how you felt</u>.

### "Best-est" Friends

A good beginning makes the reader want to know more.

Sometimes "best" just isn't good enough. On that breezy October day, the day Kerri moved away, I was crushed. Last fall, she moved with her family to Massachusetts. But now it was a year later, and she was back for the first time. Would we still be friends? Was she taller? Was I? Maybe she would be "too cool" for her old best friend.

Writer reveals her feelings.

I sat nervously on the front stoop, trying not to look too eager. Then their car pulled up, and I noticed they still had their Georgia license plates. The car door opened. Kerri stepped out hesitantly. Everything seemed to stand still and quiet for a moment. Then at the same time, we both started running toward each other.

A quotation makes the narrative lively and authentic.

"Jaysie!" she cried. "I missed you so much, my best-est friend!" Later, they moved back here. But the year apart showed me just how strong our friendship is.

# Regular and Irregular Plural Nouns

**Plural nouns** name more than one person, place, or thing.

- Most plural nouns are formed by adding -*s*.
  picture/pictures   wing/wings   day/days

- Add -*es* to nouns ending in *ch, sh, x, z, s,* and *ss*.
  bunch/bunches   wish/wishes   box/boxes   class/classes

- If a noun ends in a consonant and *y*, change *y* to *i* and add -*es*.
  berry/berries   spy/spies

- Some nouns have **irregular plural** forms. They change spelling.
  mouse/mice   goose/geese   child/children   woman/women

- For most nouns that end in *f* or *fe*, change *f* to *v* and add -*es*.
  leaf/leaves   knife/knives   calf/calves   wife/wives

- Some nouns have the same singular and plural forms.
  sheep   deer   moose   headquarters   series   elk

- For compound nouns, make only the important word plural.
  fathers-in-law   secretaries of state

- If a noun ends in a vowel and *o*, add -*s*.
  video/videos   radio/radios

- Check a dictionary for plurals of nouns ending in consonant -*o*.
  photo/photos   potato/potatoes   hero/heroes   echo/echoes

**A** Write the plural form of each singular noun. Use a dictionary
if you need help.

1. galaxy
2. planet
3. brother-in-law
4. porch
5. child

6. tomato
7. series
8. life
9. address
10. photo

**B** Write the plural forms of the underlined singular nouns.

1. <u>Man</u> who are more than 7 <u>foot</u> tall are unusual.

2. They may make better basketball <u>player</u> than <u>astronaut</u>.

3. Stars probably formed from <u>cloud</u> of <u>gas</u> and dust.

4. Do you know what black <u>hole</u> and <u>quasar</u> are?

5. There are <u>billion</u> of stars in our galaxy and <u>billion</u> of <u>galaxy</u> in the universe.

6. We took <u>sandwich</u> and <u>bunch</u> of <u>grape</u> for our <u>lunch</u>.

7. The sixth-grade <u>class</u> sat on <u>bench</u> at the planetarium.

8. The first astronauts' <u>life</u> were changed by their <u>flight</u> into space.

9. Was that a herd of <u>moose</u> or <u>elk</u>?

10. There have been several <u>headquarters</u> for the office of our national <u>secretary of state</u>.

**C** Write each sentence. Correct any errors in plural forms of nouns.

11. Several childs signed up for the classs in astronomy and physics.

12. Because of lightes in citys, we couldn't see most star's.

13. Some familys drive long distancs on country roadz so they can see the stars more clearly.

14. Long ago, viewerz imagined the shapes of beares, wolfs, and deers in the stars.

15. What shaps can you see in the night skys?

16. I discuss theorys about the originz of the universe with my two brother-in-laws.

# Test Preparation

Write the letter of the plural word that correctly completes each sentence.

1. I found several ____ of old newspapers.

   **A** boxs      **C** boxes
   **B** box's      **D** boxen

2. The astronauts synchronized their ____.

   **A** watches      **C** watch's
   **B** watchs      **D** watchies

3. They rented several science-fiction ____ from the store.

   **A** video      **C** videoes
   **B** videoz      **D** videos

4. Three ____ were born in April.

   **A** calfs      **C** calfes
   **B** calves      **D** calvies

5. Both the girls and the ____ enjoyed the movie.

   **A** boies      **C** boy's
   **B** boys      **D** boyz

6. The spaceship was split into two ____.

   **A** halves      **C** halfs
   **B** halvs      **D** halfes

7. What ____ support the space program?

   **A** industrys      **C** industries
   **B** industris      **D** industry's

8. New ____ grew out of space discoveries.

   **A** businesses      **C** businesss
   **B** businessies      **D** business's

9. The photo showed peaks and ____ on the planet.

   **A** valleies      **C** vallies
   **B** valleyes      **D** valleys

10. Are ____ larger than ducks?

    **A** gooses      **C** goosies
    **B** geese      **D** geeses

# Review

 Write the plural form of each singular noun.

1. democracy
2. thief
3. family
4. pass
5. woman
6. series
7. blueberry
8. sheep
9. tomato
10. mother-in-law
11. church
12. holiday
13. dream
14. video
15. moose
16. loaf
17. monkey
18. commander-in-chief
19. mouse
20. crash

 Write each sentence using the correct plural forms of the nouns in ( ).

21. The (children, childs) gave reports on space travel.
22. How many (galaxys, galaxies) exist in the universe?
23. We can use (telescops, telescopes) to see distant stars.
24. Astronauts are (heros, heroes) to many people.
25. In the early years, their return to Earth was celebrated with (speechs, speeches) and parades.
26. People watched the (skys, skies) with new awareness.
27. Those (days, daies) are over.
28. We are not glued to our (radioes, radios) and TV sets during space flights.
29. Still, (Americans, Americanes) are proud of our history in space.
30. The space program's (mans, men) and women have done many great things.
31. (Echos, Echoes) of the past urge us to do more in the future.
32. We hope space exploration will continue without too many big (delays, delaies).

**WRITER'S CRAFT**

# Include Important Information

Include only **important information** to make your directions concise and easy to follow. Extra or unnecessary information can interfere with meaning.

 Write the sentence in each paragraph that contains unimportant information.

1. To get to the fruit stand, walk south to Oak Street and turn left. My aunt lives on Oak Street. Go two blocks and turn left on Cherry Street. The fruit stand is on the right, halfway down the block.

2. To make pancakes, first sift flour, sugar, and salt. Then mix in eggs and water. The eggs get a little messy, though. Whisk the mixture for one minute and then pour it into a hot skillet.

3. Taking care of tropical fish requires time and careful attention. Make sure the water is the right temperature. Keep the water clean and feed the fish according to instructions. Make sure you don't put the wrong kind of fish together in the same tank! Do you have tropical fish?

4. Trace a circle on paper using a round object like the lid of a jar. Cut out the circle. Fold the circle in half and in half again. Fold it in half a third time. Make sure your hands are clean. Cut little triangles and other shapes along the fold. Unfold the paper— and it's a snowflake!

 Write directions about how to go from your house to school or another nearby location. Include only important information that someone following your directions would need to know.

# Directions

Good **directions** help readers understand what to do to get somewhere or to accomplish a task. Steps should be clear, logical, and to the point.

First sentence provides a lively introduction to the task.

Ingredients are listed in order of use.

Steps are in logical order. Transition words are used to show order.

### Out-of-This-World Banana Split

This dessert is easy to make and so good it will send you into orbit!

*Ingredients*

1 banana, peeled

2 scoops of Martian Green ice cream

whipped cream

2 tablespoons of Jupiter Berry Syrup

1 pinch of stardust (Sprinkles will do.)

First, slice the banana lengthwise and put the halves side by side in a shallow bowl. Next, place the scoops of ice cream in the center of the bowl between the two banana halves. Then beat the whipped cream rapidly. Dollop fluffy whipped-cream clouds on top of the ice cream. After that, pour the syrup slowly over the whipped cream. This should make it look like the surface of Jupiter. Finally, add a pinch of stardust. Eat while the moon is rising.

# Possessive Nouns

A **possessive noun** shows ownership. A **singular possessive noun** shows that one person, place, or thing has or owns something. A **plural possessive noun** shows that more than one person, place, or thing has or owns something.

- To make a singular noun show possession, add an apostrophe (') and -*s*.
  the ranch's landscape     James's coat
- To make a plural noun that ends in -*s* show possession, add an apostrophe (').
  five writers' collections    the bushes' leaves
- To make a plural noun that does not end in -*s* show possession, add an apostrophe (') and -*s*.
  the children's books       the women's ideas

**A** Write the possessive form of each noun. Write *S* if the possessive noun is singular. Write *P* if it is plural.

| | |
|---|---|
| **1.** computer | **11.** rock |
| **2.** Mr. Garcia | **12.** geologists |
| **3.** hornets | **13.** men |
| **4.** student | **14.** girl |
| **5.** dinosaurs | **15.** riverbank |
| **6.** fossil | **16.** storm |
| **7.** women | **17.** skeletons |
| **8.** explorers | **18.** stories |
| **9.** reptiles | **19.** dish |
| **10.** Earth | **20.** pictures |

**B** Write the correct possessive noun in ( ) to complete each sentence.

1. The (dinosaur's, dinosaurs') remains showed that it was about the size of a dog.
2. All (paleontologist's, paleontologists') work requires patience.
3. A (fossil's, fossils') condition provides clues.
4. We walked slowly as we stared at the (river's, rivers') dry bed.
5. This (field trip's, field trips') purpose was fossil hunting.
6. Several (children's, childrens') finds were new and exciting.
7. This rock has imprints of several (trilobite's, trilobites') bodies.
8. This ancient (arthropod's, arthropods') body looks like a small armored tank.
9. The (worker's, workers') days began at dawn and ended when they could no longer see.
10. The (men's, mens') and (women's, womens') muscles ached after they crouched all day.

**C** Write each sentence. Change the underlined words to a phrase with a possessive noun.

11. The project of our class on dinosaurs was interesting.
12. *Tyrannosaurus rex* was the choice of several students.
13. The report of Dylan focused on a less familiar dinosaur.
14. The dinosaur of Iris was an ancestor of the horse.
15. The apatosaurus was the suggestion of our teacher.
16. What was the climate of Earth like millions of years ago?
17. Why is the extinction of the dinosaurs so fascinating to us?
18. Like the work of detectives, paleontologists' work involves finding and interpreting clues.

# Test Preparation

✓ Write the letter of the word that correctly completes each sentence.

1. The ____ waters were the home for the first living things.

   **A** oceans    **C** oceans's
   **B** ocean    **D** oceans'

2. This ____ display of dinosaur fossils is excellent.

   **A** museum's
   **B** museums'
   **C** museums's
   **D** museums

3. Millions of years ago, an ____ body was trapped in tree sap.

   **A** insects    **C** insects'
   **B** insect's    **D** insect

4. Please look at ____ book on fossils.

   **A** Briannas'
   **B** Briannas
   **C** Brianna's
   **D** Brianna

5. That ____ substance is neither bone nor rock.

   **A** fossils'
   **B** fossil
   **C** fossil's
   **D** fossils

6. The ____ bodies were preserved in a rock called amber.

   **A** beetle's    **C** beetles's
   **B** beetles'    **D** beetle

7. ____ newest project is a dig in West Africa.

   **A** Dr. Liakos's
   **B** Dr. Liakos'
   **C** Dr. Liakoss
   **D** Dr. Liakos

8. He must have the ____ permission before he begins digging.

   **A** governments
   **B** government's
   **C** governments's
   **D** government

9. All ____ reports must be supported by facts.

   **A** archaeologists
   **B** archaeologistes
   **C** archaeologist's
   **D** archaeologists'

10. Last year two ____ claims were proven false.

    **A** mens'    **C** men's
    **B** man's    **D** mans'

# Review

 Write the possessive form of each noun. Write *S* if the possessive noun is singular. Write *P* if it is plural.

1. canyon
2. floods
3. child
4. rains
5. sciences
6. asteroid
7. hillsides
8. stories
9. paintbrush
10. men

11. man
12. geese
13. weather
14. Chris
15. reporters
16. mice
17. women
18. children
19. Mr. Harris
20. camp

 Write the correct possessive noun in ( ) to complete each sentence.

21. A (bird's, birds') bones are hollow.
22. These (dinosaur's, dinosaurs') bones are also hollow.
23. (Ms. Rausch's, Ms. Rauschs') belief is that birds and dinosaurs shared a common ancestor.
24. One (fossil's, fossils') discovery sheds light on this theory.
25. A (pterodactyl's, pterodactyls') arms were like wings.
26. A membrane stretched across both (arm's, arms') bones.
27. These (creature's, creatures') bodies had birdlike beaks and tails.
28. Their (bodies, bodies') adaptations allowed pteradactyls to fly.
29. It was a primitive bird in a (dinosaur's, dinosaurs') body.
30. Many (reptile's, reptiles') characteristics remind us of dinosaurs.
31. There are no dinosaurs in (today's, todays') world.
32. A (human's, humans') legs couldn't run fast enough to escape those jaws!

# Posing Questions

> **Posing questions** can help you focus your writing. As you develop your topic, answer questions that your reader might ask.

 Which question would better help you write about the given topic? Write the letter of the question.

1. *Topic:* The solar system and life
   - **A** Why is there life on Earth but not on Venus?
   - **B** How many planets are there?

2. *Topic:* The extinction of dinosaurs
   - **A** Why did few dinosaurs survive the Ice Age?
   - **B** Where are most fossils found?

3. *Topic:* Careers in science
   - **A** How many years of school do you need to be a scientist?
   - **B** How is a science career different from other professions?

4. *Topic:* The effects of volcanic activity on Earth
   - **A** Are volcanic eruptions frequent?
   - **B** How does a volcanic eruption change the surface of our planet?

5. *Topic:* Water pollution and fish
   - **A** How do waterways become polluted?
   - **B** What kinds of fish are no longer found in our polluted rivers?

6. *Topic:* Science experiments and safety
   - **A** Where do labs purchase their chemical supplies?
   - **B** How can you protect yourself in the lab?

 Write two questions about the following topic.

   *Topic:* Insects are eating our crops.

# Hypothesis and Results

A **hypothesis** is something assumed to be true that you intend to prove or disprove with the **results** of research or an experiment. Your argument needs to be clear and well supported with facts.

Writer makes a hypothesis.

Results support the hypothesis.

Transition words connect sentences.

### Dinosaurs Are Not Lizards!

Scientists once thought that dinosaurs were giant reptiles. The name *dinosaur* actually means "terrible lizard." However, this idea may not be true. The more scientists studied the two kinds of animals, the more they began to notice big differences between dinosaurs and reptiles. There are differences in bone structure and teeth. There are differences in their social life—some dinosaurs hunted in packs, while reptiles tend to hunt alone. Some paleontologists even think that dinosaurs were warm-blooded. Reptiles are cold-blooded. Though nothing is yet completely certain, it's probably true that while dinosaurs were "terrible," they were not "lizards" after all.

# Action and Linking Verbs

A **verb** is the main word in the predicate of a sentence. The verb tells what the subject of the sentence is or does. An **action verb** tells what the subject does. A **linking verb** links, or joins, the subject with a word or words in the predicate that tell what the subject is or is like. Linking verbs are most often forms of the verb *be*, such as *am, is, are, was*, and *were*. *Become, seem, appear, feel, taste, smell*, and *look* can be linking verbs.

| | |
|---|---|
| **Action Verbs** | Girls <u>place</u> bonnets on their heads. |
| | She <u>walks</u> down the path. |
| **Linking Verbs** | They <u>seem</u> awkward in their bonnets. |
| | The boy <u>is</u> happy. |

- A **predicate nominative** is a noun or pronoun that follows a linking verb and identifies or explains the subject: *The mattresses were straw-filled <u>bags</u>. This bed is <u>mine</u>.*

**A** Write *A* if the underlined word is an action verb. Write *L* if it is a linking verb. Write *PN* if it is a predicate nominative.

1. Charles is a <u>blacksmith</u>.
2. Darlene <u>was</u> proud of her homemade pie.
3. The milk <u>splashed</u> on the floor.
4. The baked ham <u>smells</u> good.
5. Uncle Joslin <u>carried</u> water in buckets.
6. The girls <u>laundered</u> the clothes.
7. Billy is a blacksmith's <u>apprentice</u>.
8. The boys <u>owned</u> many books.
9. The girls <u>practiced</u> their sewing.
10. The straw mattresses <u>felt</u> hard and lumpy.

**B** Write the verb in each sentence. Write *A* if it is an action verb. Write *L* if it is a linking verb.

1. In the 1800s, many families lived in the country.
2. Most men were farmers.
3. They raised crops and livestock.
4. Women worked hard in the home.
5. In old pictures, the children appear happy.
6. However, they did many chores every day.
7. Now we buy almost everything in stores.
8. We no longer make our own bread, butter, and soap.
9. Some of these skills seem amazing to us now.
10. Less work and more leisure are ours today.

**C** Add a verb of your own to complete each sentence. Write the sentence. Write *A* or *L* to tell what kind of verb you added.

11. That large tin pan ____ a bathtub.
12. Bathers ____ in and poured water over themselves.
13. People ____ water for a bath over the fire.
14. Farmers ____ crops for food.
15. Horses, mules, or oxen ____ plows in the fields.
16. Children ____ school but not during planting or harvesting season.
17. No phones, radios, or TVs ____ in the house.
18. Their world ____ quiet.
19. Children ____ few toys.
20. Young people ____ the skills of adult life.

# Test Preparation

✓ Write the letter of the word that is an action verb.

**1.** Edgar carried water from the stream to the house.

   **A** Edgar    **C** stream
   **B** carried    **D** house

**2.** Betsy baked bread although she was tired.

   **A** baked    **C** was
   **B** although    **D** tired

**3.** Father and Ben milked cows morning and evening.

   **A** Ben    **C** morning
   **B** cows    **D** milked

**4.** The children studied their lessons by candlelight.

   **A** children    **C** studied
   **B** lessons    **D** their

✓ Write the letter of the word that is a linking verb.

**5.** A horse and wagon were yesterday's car.

   **A** horse    **C** were
   **B** A    **D** and

**6.** The fresh, baked bread smelled wonderful.

   **A** baked    **C** fresh
   **B** bread    **D** smelled

**7.** The big meal they ate at noon tasted delicious.

   **A** big    **C** tasted
   **B** ate    **D** delicious

**8.** Their clothing appeared stiff and uncomfortable.

   **A** Their    **C** appeared
   **B** clothing    **D** stiff

**9.** Plenty of food is necessary for energy.

   **A** is    **C** energy
   **B** food    **D** for

**10.** The homemade soap looked thick and yellow.

   **A** and    **C** thick
   **B** soap    **D** looked

# Review

Write *A* if the underlined word is an action verb. Write *L* if it is a linking verb. Write *PN* if it is a predicate nominative.

1. Belle <u>dropped</u> hot coals into the iron.
2. The kitchen <u>was</u> terribly hot.
3. The blacksmith <u>hammered</u> red-hot iron.
4. His shop <u>seemed</u> like an oven.
5. Clyde <u>cut</u> the weeds with a scythe.
6. The women <u>sewed</u> all the clothes by hand.
7. James became the blacksmith's <u>helper</u>.
8. He <u>appeared</u> happy with his teacher.
9. The people in old-time clothes are <u>actors</u>.
10. That cornshuck bed <u>looks</u> lumpy.

Write the verb in each sentence.
Write *A* if the verb is an action verb.
Write *L* if it is a linking verb.

11. Nan sewed a sampler.
12. The stitches seemed impossibly small and even.
13. The men made sausage.
14. It tasted fresh and delicious.
15. The horses neighed a greeting.
16. Ralph forked hay into their stalls.
17. Bedtime was soon after supper.
18. Everyone rose with the sun.
19. The new day's work began before breakfast.
20. They ate hearty meals for energy.
21. I am grateful for today's conveniences.
22. Our ancestors worked very hard.

**WRITER'S CRAFT**

# Parallel Structure

> If a sentence has parts that are alike, those parts should have the same form or pattern.
>
> **Parallel structure** refers to the pattern, or organization, of similar sentence parts, such as verbs and adjectives.
>
> **Not Parallel**   Fish swim, birds fly, and barking is something that dogs do.
>
> **Parallel**   Fish swim, birds fly, and dogs bark.

 Write the letter of the parallel sentence in each pair.

**1. A**   We asked if we could run, play, and wrestling.

   **B**   We asked if we could run, play, and wrestle.

**2. A**   Lydia went to a ballgame, a concert, and a movie.

   **B**   Lydia went to a ballgame, a concert, and saw a movie.

**3. A**   My dog is hungry, thirsty, and sleepy.

   **B**   My dog is hungry, wants a drink, and to sleep.

**4. A**   Hank looked across the field and was walking toward the barn.

   **B**   Hank looked across the field and walked toward the barn.

 Rewrite the sentences in this paragraph to make them parallel.

One morning I got up, put on my clothes, eating my breakfast, and walked outside. When I reached the street, I saw a red car, a blue truck, and a motorcycle that was yellow. I waited for the light, stepped off the curb, and across the street.

# Friendly Letter

A **friendly letter** begins with a salutation, such as *Dear ...,* and ends with a closing, such as *Sincerely,* and a signature. The body of the letter may have news, descriptions, opinions, questions, and explanations—anything that would appeal to a friend. The letter is written in an informal voice.

**A Letter to Thomas**

November 3, 2 _____

Letter begins with date and salutation.

Dear Thomas,

How are things in the 1800s? I can't imagine what it must be like without electricity, although I think using candles and cooking on a hearth sound like fun. Let me tell you about my life in the 2000s.

Voice of letter is friendly and informal.

I play basketball after school. It is a team sport in which you throw a ball through a hoop overhead.

Writer provides information about modern activities and inventions.

I also use my computer, which is a machine that provides information instantly! It helped me learn what life was like during your time. I can also play chess and design pictures on it. In fact, I'm using it to write you this letter!

Well, I must go now. It's getting late, and I have to turn lights off at 9:30. Lights are like candles that can make a room bright with a flick of a switch. I'll write again soon.

Letter ends with closing and signature.

Your friend,
Arthur

# Subject-Verb Agreement

The subject and verb in a sentence must **agree,** or work together. A singular subject needs a singular verb. A plural subject needs a plural verb. Use these rules for verbs that express present time.

- If the subject is a singular noun or *he, she,* or *it,* add *-s* or *-es* to most verbs.

  The planet *glows.* The scientist *teaches* school. One of the students *takes* notes. He *works* hard.

- If the subject is compound, a plural noun, or *I, you, we,* or *they,* do not add *-s* or *-es* to the verb.

  The planets *glow.* The scientist and the assistant *teach* school. Several of the students *take* notes. They *work* hard.

- For the verb *be,* use *am* and *is* to agree with singular subjects and *are* to agree with plural subjects.

  I *am* a scientist. My father *is* on the moon.

  The planets *are* visible. We *are* on Earth.

- A **collective noun** names a group, such as *family, team,* and *class.* A collective noun is singular if it refers to a group acting as one: The class *is waiting* for takeoff. A collective noun is plural if it refers to members of the group acting individually: The class *are choosing* their seats.

A  Write *Yes* if the subject and the verb in the sentence agree. If they do not agree, write *No.*

 1. A shaft of light blinds me.
 2. Supplies costs the settlers more on the moon.
 3. The group understands the importance of water.
 4. The ferry move slowly from its loading dock.
 5. The kids on the moon is having a party.

**B** Write the verb in ( ) that agrees with the subject.

1. Your moon weight (are, is) one-sixth of your Earth weight.
2. The moon (has, have) a smaller force of gravity than Earth.
3. Less gravity (make, makes) the moon's atmosphere very thin.
4. Visitors to the moon (need, needs) their own oxygen and water.
5. They (leap, leaps) much farther on the moon.
6. (Are, Is) moon rocks valuable?
7. The astronauts (wear, wears) spacesuits.
8. A suit (protect, protects) a moon visitor from extremes of temperature and lack of oxygen.
9. (Think, Thinks) of the future in space.
10. (Are, Is) cities thriving on the moon?

**C** Write a complete sentence using the noun or pronoun as the subject and the correct form of the verb.

11. planets (revolve, revolves)
12. we (live, lives)
13. sun (provide, provides)
14. people (need, needs)
15. one of the planets (is, are)
16. scientists (discover, discovers)
17. astronomers (observe, observes)
18. I (see, sees)
19. stars (look, looks)
20. they (is, are)

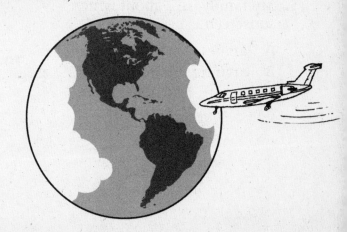

# Test Preparation

✓ Write the letter of the verb that agrees with the subject in each sentence.

1. Our Sun ____ a star.

   A  is          C  be
   B  are         D  am

2. It ____ tremendous heat and light.

   A  generate'   C  generating
   B  generate    D  generates

3. Energy from the sun ____ Earth's atmosphere.

   A  entering    C  enter
   B  enters      D  enter's

4. Ultraviolet light ____ your skin.

   A  harming     C  harms'
   B  harms        D  harm

5. My family ____ about which sunscreen is best.

   A  argues      C  argue's
   B  arguing     D  argue

6. Only a small part of the spectrum of light ____ visible.

   A  am          C  are
   B  being       D  is

7. Rainbows ____ us the colors that make up visible light.

   A  show        C  shows
   B  showing     D  show's

8. X-rays and gamma rays ____ light waves you cannot see.

   A  be          C  is
   B  are         D  am

9. They ____ a higher frequency, or number of waves per second.

   A  has         C  haves
   B  have        D  has'

10. The study of light ____ me.

    A  interesting  C  interests
    B  interest's   D  interest

# Review

Write *Yes* if the subject and verb in the sentence agree. If they do not agree, write *No* and the correct form of the verb.

1. Experts debate the best way of travel for the future.
2. We depends heavily on automobiles.
3. Trains has become less popular.
4. Airlines struggles with high fuel prices.
5. Pollution from engines threatens our air.
6. Hybrid cars burn less gasoline.
7. Their engines uses both electric and gas power.
8. High-speed rail offer fast, efficient travel.
9. Millions of people zoom along at 150–200 miles per hour on European and Japanese trains.
10. A much faster magnetic train are in the works.
11. A team at Cal Tech is developing an all-electric car.
12. This kind of car reduce our dependence on oil.

 Complete each sentence using the correct form of the verb or verbs in ( ). Write each sentence.

13. Pieter (enter) his personal travel pod.
14. It (operate) on a fuel made from hydrogen.
15. Millions of pods (run) on invisible electronic tracks in the sky.
16. They (move) people to and from work and school.
17. This form of transportation (travel) at a high speed and (produce) no pollution.
18. The pod's computer (know) the route and (guide) the vehicle.
19. Electronic sensors on the pod (prevent) collisions.
20. These vehicles of the future (be) not just an engineer's fantasy.

# Dialogue

> **Dialogue** is a character's actual words. Dialogue is placed inside quotation marks in a story but written without quotation marks in a play or an interview. Good dialogue reveals a character's thoughts and attitudes.

 Match each quotation to the appropriate sentence below. (Note the punctuation for each.) Write the sentence, including the quotation.

"Wow! You never told me North Carolina would look like this!"

"that is, unless you bring me lunch."

"How can I make this choice?"

"so how did we end up with a snake?"

"Oh, dear, not again,"

"and away we go!"

1. _____ he asked, looking at the two doors.

2. "You're not allowed to visit football practice," Tania told her mother, _____

3. The pilot seemed very excited. "Just one push of the button," he exclaimed, _____

4. _____ said Ralphie, his eyes full of wonder.

5. _____ sighed Sophia, dejected. "We ran out of peanut butter."

6. "You said you were buying a hamster," said Bonnie, _____

Imagine you are writing a brief scene in a story. Larry has given Mari an unexpected gift. Write Mari's response as dialogue. Her words should show whether she thinks the gift is weird or wonderful.

# Interview

> An **interview** is a question-and-answer discussion with someone. A good interviewer asks questions that call for thoughtful responses, not just a *yes* or *no*.

First question gives reader background information.

Details give a vivid picture of the future.

Interviewer asks follow-up questions to provide insights.

**Interview with Futura Bolden by Marla McCoy**

**MM:** Futura, you're my age, but you come from the future. What is it like in your time?

**FB:** Well, it's very different. We use turbo shoes, not cars, to get around. Our fruits and vegetables are grown in cube-shapes for easier storage.

**MM:** Doesn't this affect the taste?

**FB:** I suppose they have less flavor, but they're much neater and more convenient.

**MM:** What is school like in the future?

**FB:** It's pretty much the same as your school. However, we start at 4:00 A.M. and get a day off for Moon Colony Day.

**MM:** Do you think you are getting a good education?

**FB:** Yes, we concentrate on math, science, and literature, which are important life skills.

**MM:** Why is literature an important life skill?

**FB:** Learning how people coped and succeeded in other times is necessary for survival.

**MM:** Well, Futura, thanks for the interview.

**FB:** You're welcome. Take the Time Travel Transit and visit me anytime.

# Past, Present, and Future Tenses

The **tense** of a verb shows when something happens. **Present tense** verbs show action that happens now. Most present tense singular verbs end with *-s*. Most present tense plural verbs do not.

Marge <u>picks</u> flowers from the garden. They <u>pick</u> flowers.

**Past tense** verbs show action that has already happened. Most verbs in the past tense end in *-ed*.

The flowers in the vase <u>wilted</u> after two days.

**Future tense** verbs show action that will happen. Add *will* (or *shall*) to most verbs to show the future tense.

Flowers with no water <u>will wilt</u> soon.

Some regular verbs change spelling when *-ed* is added. For verbs ending in *e*, drop the *e* and add *-ed*: *liked, baked.* For verbs ending in a consonant and *y*, change the *y* to *i* and add *-ed*: *hurried, carried.*

For most one-syllable verbs that end in one vowel followed by one consonant, double the consonant and add *-ed*: *stopped, bragged.*

Irregular verbs change spelling to form the past tense: *are/were, break/broke, bring/brought, build/built, buy/bought, do/did, find/found, go/went, have/had, is/was, keep/kept, make/made, sit/sat, see/saw, take/took, teach/taught, tell/told, wear/wore, write/wrote.*

**A** Identify the tense of each verb. Write *present, past,* or *future.*

1. noted      4. explains      7. discovered
2. tell       5. shipped       8. will teach
3. will study 6. saw

**B** For each present tense verb below, write the past tense and the future tense forms.

1. make
2. are
3. find
4. design
5. harvest
6. live
7. play
8. build
9. believe
10. go

11. write
12. is
13. keep
14. grab
15. have
16. teach
17. survive
18. buy
19. worry
20. survey

**C** Complete each sentence. Use a verb in the tense indicated in ( ) and other words. Write the sentence.

21. (past) Ancient Egyptian writing ____
22. (present) Experts on Egyptology ____
23. (future) Future generations ____
24. (past) A word picture, or hieroglyph, ____
25. (future) The King Tut exhibit ____
26. (past) This ancient Egyptian pharaoh ____
27. (present) Today people all over the world ____
28. (future) Archaeologists who are interested in ancient Egypt ____

# Test Preparation

✓ Write the letter of the verb that correctly completes each sentence.

1. Long ago, Egyptians ___ paper from papyrus.

   A  make
   B  made
   C  are making
   D  will make

2. Now sixth graders ___ ancient cultures in social studies.

   A  study
   B  studying
   C  will studied
   D  will studying

3. Next week they ___ a mural about ancient Egypt.

   A  draw
   B  drawing
   C  will draw
   D  drew

4. Yesterday Jan ___ the class about the pyramids.

   A  tells
   B  told
   C  is telling
   D  will tell

✓ Write the letter of the past tense form of the underlined verb.

5. Workers <u>lift</u> the enormous stones onto the pyramid.

   A  lifted
   B  were lifted
   C  lifting
   D  will lift

6. Men and women <u>wear</u> linen skirts or robes.

   A  is wear
   B  are wearing
   C  weared
   D  wore

7. In 1922, archaeologists <u>uncover</u> the tomb of King Tut.

   A  will uncover
   B  uncovered
   C  are uncovering
   D  will uncovered

8. They <u>keep</u> a careful record of precious objects in the tomb.

   A  kept
   B  will keep
   C  keeped
   D  were keep

# Review

Identify the tense of each underlined verb. Write *present, past,* or *future.*

1. Tigers once <u>roamed</u> in California.
2. We <u>see</u> models of them in the La Brea museum.
3. These saber-toothed tigers <u>were</u> fierce predators.
4. They no longer <u>exist</u> except in our imagination.
5. Which animals <u>will disappear</u> in the next thousand years?
6. Today's animals <u>bear</u> a resemblance to some ancient animals.
7. Wooly mammoths <u>looked</u> like our elephants.
8. What <u>will</u> future generations <u>think</u> of our animals?
9. Ancient Egyptians <u>loved</u> games and outdoor activities.
10. They <u>had</u> pets such as monkeys and cats.

For each present tense verb below, write the past tense and the future tense forms.

11. bring
12. take
13. hurry
14. see
15. have
16. tell
17. break
18. teach
19. roast
20. wear

21. keep
22. find
23. buy
24. write
25. go
26. stop
27. build
28. do
29. sit
30. bake

# Style

You express a personal style in the way you dress, talk, and write. **Style** is the quality that makes a piece of writing memorable and distinct. To develop a unique style, choose vivid words and images and vary the kinds and lengths of sentences.

 Write the letter of the phrase that describes the style of each paragraph.

- **A** Many vivid words and images
- **B** Varied sentence kinds and structures
- **C** Short, choppy sentences

1. I'm up early. Soon I'm at work. All day I drag stones uphill. Work on the new pyramid is hard. By evening I'm tired.

2. My friends think I'm crazy, but I like working on the pyramid. It's a great workout! Sure, it's exhausting when I lift those heavy boulders. But I don't mind. I work outside, get an hour for lunch, and ride home on the ox cart. What's not to like?

3. Women wore sparkly purple eye shadow. Their bright gold ankle bracelets clanked when they walked. On their heads were cones of animal fat that melted, drenching them in perfume.

 Change words and revise sentences in the following paragraph to improve the style

   The men went into the desert. They discovered a tomb. They found a room full of things. They were excited. They wrapped their findings and left.

# Writing for Tests

Imagine that a <u>person from another era</u> is visiting you. Think of an <u>important place</u> you would show your visitor. Write an <u>explanation</u> of what this place would tell your visitor about <u>your culture</u>.

## The More Things Change ...

Topic sentence sets the theme.

If I had a visitor from ancient Egypt, I would take him to see the Kansas City Airport. There, my friend would see that although many things are different now, some things are still the same.

Varied sentence structure keeps reader engaged.

All the machines, such as planes, cars, and escalators, would show how the world has changed to a more industrial society. And what would he think of people typing on portable computers while they waited for their planes? I would have to explain that computers had replaced scribes. "Hungry?" I'd say. Then we'd stop at a fast food place where I'd introduce him to his first cheeseburger. Before long, he'd realize that things move very fast in the 21st century!

Strong word choice paints a picture for the reader.

At the same time, the farms outside the city and the huge airport construction projects might seem familiar to my ancient Egyptian guest. Peaceful rows of golden, rippling grain would make him feel right at home. Sweaty workers putting together a massive new terminal might remind him of building the pyramids!

# Principal Parts of Regular Verbs

A verb's tenses are made from four basic forms. These basic forms are called the verb's **principal parts.**

| Present | Present Participle | Past | Past Participle |
|---------|--------------------|------|-----------------|
| walk | *(is, are)* walking | walked | *(has, have, had)* walked |
| study | *(is, are)* studying | studied | *(has, have, had)* studied |

A **regular verb** forms its past and past participle by adding *-d* or *-ed* to the present form.

The present and the past form can be used by themselves as verbs.

The present participle and the past participle are always used with a helping verb.

**A** Write *present, present participle, past,* or *past participle* to identify the principal part used to form the underlined verb.

1. The porcupine <u>terrified</u> the young boy.

2. Brian <u>is pouring</u> the water onto the flames.

3. Wendy <u>had wished</u> for an early spring.

4. Jack <u>saves</u> his strength.

5. The sun <u>warmed</u> his back.

6. The rescue pilots <u>are searching</u> the area every day.

7. Marian <u>carries</u> the supplies by herself.

8. The hikers <u>had settled</u> into a daily routine.

9. The hungry flames <u>are burning</u> the dry bark.

10. He <u>hammered</u> the rock with the flat end of his hatchet.

**B** Write the form of the underlined verb indicated in ( ).

1. The scouts <u>enjoy</u> a hiking trip in July each year. (present)

2. This year they <u>travel</u> to Shawnee National Forest. (present participle)

3. Last year they <u>hike</u> in the Adirondack Mountains. (past)

4. The scoutmaster <u>rent</u> a van for the gear. (past participle with *had*)

5. The group <u>cook</u> food over an open fire. (present)

6. Everyone <u>request</u> stew for dinner. (past participle with *has*)

7. Jonah's feet <u>blister</u> on the third day. (past)

8. Dan <u>develop</u> a rash from poison ivy. (past participle with *has*)

9. The scouts <u>listen</u> to scary stories around the fire at night. (present)

10. Every boy <u>pack</u> a flashlight. (past participle with *had*)

11. The troop leader <u>praise</u> the boys for their efforts. (present)

12. They <u>plan</u> a trip to Yellowstone next year. (present participle)

**C** Write a sentence using the subject and verb given. Use the form of the verb in ( ).

13. children wander (past)

14. they ignore (past participle with *have*)

15. forest look (present)

16. father search (present participle)

17. animals live (present)

18. rescuers locate (past)

19. they wait (past participle with *had*)

20. deer and raccoons visit (present participle)

# Test Preparation

Mark the letter that indicates the correct form of the underlined verb.

**1.** Spelunkers <u>explore</u> caves of all kinds.

  **A** Present
  **B** Present participle
  **C** Past
  **D** Past participle

**2.** They <u>are entering</u> the cave with their equipment.

  **A** Present
  **B** Present participle
  **C** Past
  **D** Past participle

**3.** The temperature <u>drops</u> quickly at lower depths.

  **A** Present
  **B** Present participle
  **C** Past
  **D** Past participle

**4.** Many people <u>have searched</u> these caves.

  **A** Present
  **B** Present participle
  **C** Past
  **D** Past participle

**5.** They <u>mapped</u> the network of tunnels and caverns.

  **A** Present
  **B** Present participle
  **C** Past
  **D** Past participle

**6.** Millions of tourists <u>visited</u> national parks last year.

  **A** Present
  **B** Present participle
  **C** Past
  **D** Past participle

**7.** The caves <u>are attracting</u> many people each year.

  **A** Present
  **B** Present participle
  **C** Past
  **D** Past participle

**8.** Elevators <u>carry</u> guides and tourists down hundreds of feet.

  **A** Present
  **B** Present participle
  **C** Past
  **D** Past participle

# Review

Write *present, present participle, past,* or *past participle* to identify the principal part used to form the underlined verb.

1. Our science class <u>is learning</u> about fire.
2. Fuel, oxygen, and a spark <u>combine</u>.
3. The teacher <u>is striking</u> a match.
4. What <u>caused</u> the spark?
5. Maria <u>used</u> a flint and a steel file.
6. The sparks <u>bounced</u> several feet.
7. A magnifying glass also <u>works</u>.
8. The glass <u>concentrated</u> the sun's rays.
9. Sean <u>had gathered</u> some soft, dry moss and twigs.
10. Cloth <u>starts</u> a fire most efficiently.
11. Mr. Gottfried <u>had charred</u> rags in a tin.
12. We <u>learned</u> fire safety rules too.

Write the form of the underlined verb indicated in ( ).

13. Natives <u>fish</u> in the river with spears. (past)
14. They <u>construct</u> houses of wood and mud. (past)
15. Yolanda and Paul <u>report</u> about tribes of the Northwest. (past participle with *have*)
16. Yesterday they <u>carve</u> a wooden owl. (past)
17. Now they <u>weave</u> a basket from bark. (present participle)
18. Jaron <u>gather</u> berries for lunch. (present)
19. Carissa <u>cook</u> a fish over the fire. (past participle with *has*)
20. The campers <u>enjoy</u> this wilderness meal. (present participle)

# Thesis Statement

A **thesis statement** is the main idea of an essay. It expresses the writer's point of view. For example, if you are asked to write about nutrition, your thesis statement might be *A healthy diet will help you live longer*. Other points in your essay should support your thesis statement.

What's your favorite sport? (No thesis)

Our school should create a new soccer field. (Thesis statement)

For each paragraph below, write the letter of the appropriate thesis statement.

**A** Wild bears must be protected.

**B** Wild bears are dangerous!

1. You hear stories of campers who have been chased away by wild bears. Some people think bears will leave you alone if you don't bother them. However, if you don't properly store your food, a bear is likely to enter your campsite. Bears are big and strong and could easily harm you if you're not careful.

2. I am writing to you, Senator, to ask for your help. The wild bears in our state are running out of room. We need to set aside some land for a national park. That way, bears can roam free without invading nearby towns.

Write a thesis statement and conclusion on the topic of pet care, based on the following details.

Pets need shelter, food, and water, just like we do. When they are sick, animals need care and treatment. Pets get lonely too. It's not fair to keep your pet tied up or locked in a room all the time.

# Expository Writing

**Expository writing** is based on information. Sometimes the goal of expository writing is to share information or ideas. However, a writer may also use information to support an opinion. Writers who feel strongly about an issue should make their position clear from the beginning and use convincing examples and facts.

**Campfires: Keep a Watchful Eye**

Thesis statement introduces the subject and expresses the writer's opinion.

Campfires present a real danger to our national forests, so campers need to be very careful. Though campfires are an essential part of the camping experience, unattended campfires have caused countless forest fires over the years. You may think your campfire is too small to spread to the forest around you, but watch out! Dry leaves and needles on the forest floor can burn quickly. Wind can pick up speed and spread your fire thirty feet before you know it. All it takes is one flyaway spark, and your campfire can cause acres of damage. So always keep an eye on your campfire and make sure you have plenty of water nearby, just in case. A watchful eye is the best way to protect our precious forests.

Main body supports the thesis.

Conclusion sums everything up.

# Principal Parts of Irregular Verbs

Usually you add *-ed* to a verb to show past tense. **Irregular verbs** do not follow this rule. Instead of having *-ed* forms to show past tense, irregular verbs usually change to other words.

| Present | Present Participle *(is, are)* | Past | Past Participle *(has, have, had)* |
|---|---|---|---|
| become | becoming | became | become |
| choose | choosing | chose | chosen |
| fall | falling | fell | fallen |
| find | finding | found | found |
| get | getting | got | gotten |
| give | giving | gave | given |
| go | going | went | gone |
| hear | hearing | heard | heard |
| is/are | being | was/were | been |
| know | knowing | knew | known |
| leave | leaving | left | left |
| sing | singing | sang | sung |
| speak | speaking | spoke | spoken |

**A** Write *present, present participle, past,* or *past participle* to identify the principal part used to form the underlined verb.

1. Marian <u>chose</u> her favorite songs.
2. Eleanor Roosevelt <u>had heard</u> about her struggles.
3. Everyone <u>knows</u> the story of Marian Anderson.
4. She <u>is giving</u> the performance of her life.
5. The audience <u>knew</u> Marian's strong, velvety voice.
6. The crowd <u>is speaking</u> in whispers.
7. Ethel May <u>had become</u> Marian's biggest fan.
8. They <u>go</u> to Europe next week.

**B** Write the verb in ( ) that correctly completes each sentence.

1. After the concert, Dana (knowed, knew) her future career.
2. Soon she (had chosen, choosed) a voice teacher.
3. Every day she (leaved, left) home at 6:30 for the train.
4. Ms. Rossi (is giving, gaved) her voice lessons.
5. No one (are singing, sings) as beautifully as Ms. Rossi.
6. Thousands of fans (going, went) to her concerts over the years.
7. In three months, Dana (sung, had sung) thousands of scales and exercises.
8. After all the practice, she (hears, hearing) a change in her voice.
9. Every day, she (finded, is finding) singing easier.
10. Last week, Ms. Rossi (getted, got) her new music for the spring recital.

**C** Write a sentence using the principal part of the given verb indicated in ( ).

11. go (present participle with *are*)
12. hear (past participle with *have*)
13. sing (present)
14. know (past)
15. become (past participle with *has*)
16. give (past)
17. speak (present)
18. fall (past participle with *had*)
19. get (present participle with *is*)
20. leave (past)

# Test Preparation

✓ Write the letter of the verb that completes each sentence.

1. Mom ____ to the opera last night.

   A  goes
   B  goed
   C  went
   D  has gone

2. The performers ____ in Italian.

   A  is singing
   B  are singing
   C  singed
   D  singing

3. Brian ____ a book about opera.

   A  choosed
   B  have chosed
   C  choose
   D  has chosen

4. The costumes ____ very detailed.

   A  is
   B  are
   C  are been
   D  was

5. No one ____ the theater at intermission.

   A  has leaved
   B  leaving
   C  left
   D  are leaving

6. Penny ____ some of the songs.

   A  knows
   B  knowed
   C  have knowed
   D  known

7. Complete silence ____ over the crowd.

   A  falled
   B  fallen
   C  are falling
   D  has fallen

8. Papa ____ our seats for us.

   A  find
   B  is finding
   C  finded
   D  have find

# Review

Write *present, present participle, past,* or *past participle* to identify the principal part used to form the underlined verb.

1. Carl and Susan <u>speak</u> fluent German.
2. Lynn <u>has become</u> a fan of German literature.
3. We <u>are leaving</u> for Europe on Saturday.
4. My cousins <u>have fallen</u> under the spell of Bavaria.
5. They <u>went</u> to a beautiful castle.
6. Local citizens <u>are giving</u> a performance about a king.
7. The king <u>fell</u> ill and behaved strangely.
8. He <u>left</u> little money in the country's treasury.
9. However, the castle <u>had become</u> a jeweled masterpiece.
10. Many visitors <u>find</u> their way to this wonderful place.

Write the verb in ( ) that correctly completes each sentence.

11. The audience (is becoming, becoming) restless.
12. The orchestra (choosed, has chosen) the park for a concert.
13. Darkness (fallen, fell) by eight o'clock.
14. At last the conductor (gotten, gets) up on the podium.
15. Now he (is speaking, have spoken) to the musicians.
16. They (being, have been) ready with their instruments.
17. That night the orchestra (given, gave) an inspiring performance.
18. No one (knows, knowed) the music better.
19. People (had heared, heard) something special that night.
20. Soon everyone (are leaving, had left) the park.

# Use Powerful Verbs

> **Powerful verbs** can make your writing memorable. Try to replace weak verbs and some linking verbs with action verbs to present a clearer, more vivid picture for your readers.
>
> **Weak**            I was cold. The snow was shiny.
> **More Powerful**   I shivered. The snow sparkled.

 Replace the underlined words with an action verb from the box or your own action verb. Write the sentence.

| | | | |
|---|---|---|---|
| trembles | vowed | shimmers | echoed |
| cheered | sweated | beamed | hushed |

1. The audience <u>was quiet</u> when she walked onstage.
2. The performer <u>is nervous</u>.
3. Music <u>was loud</u> in the concert hall.
4. The singer's dress <u>is shiny</u> in the darkness.
5. Musicians <u>were hot</u> under the lights.
6. After the concert, the crowd <u>was happy</u> for the band.
7. That violinist <u>looked pleased</u> as she took a bow.
8. I <u>said</u> I would see this band again next year.

 Rewrite the following sentences. Replace the underlined words with action verbs.

   When we arrived at the hotel, we <u>got</u> off the bus. Benny's feet <u>were sore</u>. Herbie <u>went</u> right up to the front desk. The hotel manager <u>was not happy</u>. Soon we <u>were</u> in our rooms. I <u>was up</u> twelve hours later feeling refreshed.

**120**  Writing

# Biographical Study

A **biographical study** is a short biography of an important or well-known person. It might be used in an encyclopedia or a magazine. A study usually tells about only the high points of the subject's life.

**Louis Armstrong (1901–1971)**

Topic sentence states importance of subject.

Louis Armstrong was one of the most important musicians in jazz history. Born in New Orleans, Louisiana, he taught himself to play the bugle when he was thirteen. During this time he lived at the Colored Waifs' Home for Boys, a local reform school. He joined Kid Ory's Brownskin Band at

Transitions show chronological order.

the age of eighteen and went on to become the world's leading Dixieland trumpet player. "Satchmo," as Armstrong was nicknamed, also had a unique singing voice. He popularized scat singing (using

An unfamiliar term is defined.

nonsense syllables).

In 1922, Armstrong moved to Chicago to join King Oliver's Creole Jazz Band. Later he played with Fletcher Henderson and other jazz legends. In later years, he became America's goodwill ambassador, playing and singing concerts all over the world. Some of his biggest song hits were "Hello, Dolly!," "Blueberry Hill," "Mack the Knife," "C'est si bon," and "What a Wonderful World."

# Verbs, Objects, and Subject Complements

A **direct object** follows an action verb and tells who or what receives the action of the verb.

Chris told a secret. (*Told* is an action verb. *Secret* is a direct object.)

An **indirect object** follows an action verb and tells to whom or what the action of the verb is done.

Chris told Bill a secret. (The indirect object *Bill* tells to whom Chris told the secret. An indirect object comes before the direct object.)

A **subject complement** follows a linking verb and tells who or what the subject is or is like.

Maggie felt <u>sick</u>. (*Felt* is a linking verb, and *sick* is a subject complement that describes Maggie.)

Maggie is the third <u>student</u> in the first row. (*Is* is a linking verb, and *student* is a subject complement telling who Maggie is.)

• A noun used as a subject complement is a predicate noun. An adjective used as a subject complement is a predicate adjective.

Ⓐ For items 1–3, write the subject complement in each sentence. For items 4–6, write the direct objects and one indirect object. Label each answer *SC, DO,* or *IO.*

**1.** The shore was rocky.

**2.** The seawater tasted salty.

**3.** The boys were the champions in sports.

**4.** Someone painted lines on the sides of the pool.

**5.** Lee kicked her legs in the water.

**6.** The instructor gave his students diving lessons after class.

**B** Write each sentence. Circle the linking verb and underline the subject complement. Write *PA* if it is a predicate adjective. Write *PN* if it is a predicate noun.

1. The water looked perfectly calm.
2. An afternoon swim seemed a good idea.
3. Unfortunately, a strong undercurrent was present.
4. The current was a forceful pull.
5. My arms and legs became heavy logs.
6. Soon I felt very afraid.
7. I was also exhausted.
8. That lifeguard looked wonderful to me!
9. Water safety is an important skill.
10. The lake water smelled fishy.
11. The surface looked muddy.
12. The lake no longer seemed the best place for a swim.

**C** Complete each sentence with a word. Write the sentence. Write *DO* if the word you added is a direct object. Write *IO* if the word you added is an indirect object.

13. Winnie gave _____ a swimming lesson.
14. She has taught _____ for years.
15. Swimming uses up the body's _____.
16. Winnie offered _____ a snack.
17. Glenn handed _____ a dry towel.
18. She wrapped _____ gratefully around her shoulders.
19. We took _____ for the upcoming swim meet.
20. Coach offered _____ a second chance to improve our times.

# Test Preparation

✅ Write the letter of the sentence that has a subject complement.

1.  **A**  Dad taught me years ago.
    **B**  At first, I was afraid of the water.
    **C**  Then I dogpaddled in shallow water.
    **D**  I avoided the deep end of the pool.

2.  **A**  The pool water was incredibly cold.
    **B**  That first leap shocked my senses.
    **C**  After several laps, I warmed up.
    **D**  Then I enjoyed the coolness of the water.

3.  **A**  We always visit the snack bar.
    **B**  Mom gives us money for a snack.
    **C**  Usually I buy an ice cream bar.
    **D**  On a hot day, it tastes wonderful.

4.  **A**  Do not swim right after you eat.
    **B**  For decades, parents said this to children.
    **C**  Today this advice seems less urgent.
    **D**  However, a rest after lunch couldn't hurt.

✅ Write the letter of the direct object of the underlined verb in the sentence.

5.  I <u>raced</u> Doug to the buoy at the end of the swim area.

    | | | | |
    |---|---|---|---|
    | **A** | I | **C** | buoy |
    | **B** | Doug | **D** | swim area |

6.  The waves <u>slapped</u> me in the face with every stroke.

    | | | | |
    |---|---|---|---|
    | **A** | stroke | **C** | me |
    | **B** | face | **D** | slapped |

7.  Ginny <u>handed</u> me a t-shirt with a fish on it.

    | | | | |
    |---|---|---|---|
    | **A** | Ginny | **C** | me |
    | **B** | fish | **D** | t-shirt |

8.  The hot sun <u>had burned</u> my shoulders badly.

    | | | | |
    |---|---|---|---|
    | **A** | shoulders | **C** | had burned |
    | **B** | sun | **D** | badly |

# Review

✓ Write the subject complement in each sentence. Write *PA* if it is a predicate adjective. Write *PN* if it is a predicate noun.

1. My brother is a lifeguard for the park district.
2. The pool becomes crowded on Saturdays.
3. The lifeguards were alert to every move.
4. One boy looked panicky in the deep water.
5. The chlorinated water smelled clean.
6. The concrete sunbathing area felt scratchy to my feet.
7. Jamahl seemed quite calm.
8. In fact, he was nervous about the meet.
9. His coach is a former state champion.
10. The meet was a huge success for our team.

✓ Write each sentence. Circle direct objects and underline any indirect objects.

11. A pelican fed its babies fish.
12. Mom and I watched the large seabirds with amusement.
13. The diving pelican catches fish in its mouth.
14. Seagulls watch us hungrily from the beach.
15. We spread a picnic on our blanket.
16. Julie throws the gulls some crusts from her sandwich.
17. A mob of gulls surrounds us almost immediately.
18. Brent frowns and gives Julie a dirty look.
19. The gulls give our party their full attention.
20. I admire their cool, calm determination.

# Eliminate Wordiness

> To make writing clear and readable, **eliminate wordiness.**
> You can replace some phrases with single words (*sadly* for *with great sadness*, *tall* for *tall in height*, or *because* for *due to the fact that*). Delete unnecessary words. Use contractions when appropriate.
>
> | | |
> |---|---|
> | **Wordy** | The reason that we will swim is because the temperature is hot. |
> | **Improved** | We'll swim because it's hot. |

Rewrite the sentences. Make the underlined phrases less wordy. Substitute or eliminate words.

1. We stayed on the beach <u>on account of</u> there were big waves.

2. He built a sand castle <u>in a skillful way</u>.

3. It was the <u>largest sand castle in size</u> I had ever seen.

4. We <u>did not</u> think <u>we would</u> have so much fun!

5. <u>With great eagerness</u>, we opened the picnic basket.

6. Unfortunately, the food smelled bad <u>due to the fact that</u> it had been in the sun all day.

Eliminate wordiness in the sentences below. Use contractions. Write the new sentences.

**(7)** I am not sure I am wearing this sweater in a correct manner.
**(8)** The reason I had it on backwards was because it did not have a label of any kind on it. **(9)** The sweater is expensive and costs a lot!
**(10)** It is blue in color. That is my favorite of all the colors.

# Rules

> **Rules** are instructions that are written to keep people informed and safe. Safety rules should be clear, simple, and easy to understand.

The most important rule is first.

Rules are numbered so they are easy to read and follow.

Rules are arranged in logical order.

**Safety Rules for Cumberland Fishing Pond**

1. NO swimming, wading, or diving is allowed.
2. Fishing licenses are required for anyone over the age of 10.
3. Children under 7 must be accompanied by an adult.
4. Stand at least 2 feet from the edge of the dock while casting.
5. Fish taken must be above the minimum size.
6. Fish under the minimum size must be released back into the pond.
7. Be careful—the dock is slippery when wet.
8. Take all garbage with you when you leave.
9. Glass bottles and containers are not permitted.
10. Do not dump unwanted live bait into the pond.
11. Load and unload equipment only in the designated areas.
12. Have fun! Thanks for coming to Cumberland Pond.

LESSON 14

# Troublesome Verbs

Some pairs of verbs are troublesome verbs because they have similar meanings or because they look alike.

| Verb | Meaning | Present | Past | Past Participle (has, have, had) |
|------|---------|---------|------|-----------------|
| sit | sit down | sit | sat | sat |
| set | put or place | set | set | set |
| lie | rest or recline | lie | lay | lain |
| lay | put or place | lay | laid | laid |
| rise | get or move up | rise | rose | risen |
| raise | lift up | raise | raised | raised |
| let | allow or permit | let | let | let |
| leave | go away | leave | left | left |
| lend | give to someone | lend | lent | lent |
| borrow | get from someone | borrow | borrowed | borrowed |
| teach | show how | teach | taught | taught |
| learn | find out | learn | learned | learned |

**A** Write the form of the underlined verb indicated in ( ).

1. She sit at the table and peeled apples. (past)
2. The sunburn raise blisters on the worker's arms. (present)
3. The rancher had lend his bulldozer to his neighbor. (past participle)
4. Juan Valdez borrow baskets from us. (past)
5. He set his boots by the side of his bed. (present)
6. In the morning, he had rise and gone back to work. (past participle)

**128** Grammar

**B** Write the verb that correctly completes the sentence. Use context to help you decide which verb is needed.

1. Can you (learn, teach) me that folk song?

2. Our class (learned, taught) about folk literature of Mexico.

3. Helen (borrowed, lent) me her book of Latin American tales.

4. I also (borrowed, lent) a book on folk art from my teacher.

5. Those books have (lain, laid) on my desk for days.

6. I accidentally (set, sat) some papers on them.

7. Then I (let, left) them there for two weeks.

8. Will you (leave, let) me have an extra day?

9. Ms. Gomez said yes and (raised, rose) my hopes.

10. If I (raise, rise) early tomorrow, I can finish the report.

11. I (sat, set) down and went right to work.

12. I (laid, lay) the assignment sheet on the counter.

**C** Complete each sentence using a form of the verb from the box. Use the tense indicated in ( ). Write the sentences.

| lie | lay | rise | raise | sit | set |
|-----|-----|------|-------|-----|-----|

13. Papa always _____ in the large chair at the head of the table. (present)

14. Mama _____ the table with the good linen and china. (past participle)

15. The bread _____ in the loaf pan. (past participle)

16. The wonderful yeasty smell _____ my spirits immediately. (past)

17. Papa _____ his newspaper aside and came to the table. (past)

18. After dinner we usually _____ down for a siesta. (present)

# Test Preparation

✓ Write the letter of the verb that correctly completes each sentence.

1. Juanita had ____ her basket down and forgotten it.

   **A** sit     **C** sat
   **B** set     **D** setted

2. The pickers ____ their baskets to the top of the ladder.

   **A** raised     **C** rise
   **B** rose     **D** risen

3. They ____ the wormy fruit fall to the ground.

   **A** leave     **C** letted
   **B** let     **D** left

4. The birds ____ their young about the fruit.

   **A** teached     **C** taught
   **B** learned     **D** learn

✓ Write the letter of the sentence that has the correct verb.

5. **A** Javier borrowed me a basket of peaches.
   **B** I sat them on the table.
   **C** Mama learned me about preserves.
   **D** I set the jars of preserves on the pantry shelf.

6. **A** The sun raises earlier each day this spring.
   **B** It does not let me lie in bed late.
   **C** Nature has learned me about my body.
   **D** I get up early and rise the window shade.

7. **A** Georgia sits under the crabapple tree at sunset.
   **B** She loaned a folding chair from us.
   **C** Has she let her place yet for the evening?
   **D** She laid in bed and thought about the vivid colors of sunset.

8. **A** An old tomcat lays in the sunshine.
   **B** He has taught every sunny spot in the house.
   **C** When the sunbeam moves, he leaves for a new spot.
   **D** Sometimes he sets with his tail wrapped around his paws.

# Review

Write the letter of the definition of the underlined verb.

| | |
|---|---|
| **1.** <u>Set</u> your baskets on the truck. | **A** has got from someone |
| **2.** <u>Raise</u> your hands over your head. | **B** has put or placed |
| **3.** June <u>has borrowed</u> a coat. | **C** gets or moves up |
| **4.** I <u>have learned</u> the job. | **D** put or place |
| **5.** The sun <u>rises</u> at 6:00 tomorrow. | **E** lift something up |
| **6.** Hakim <u>has laid</u> down his shears. | **F** have found out |

Write the form of the underlined verb indicated in ( ).

**7.** The workers <u>leave</u> for the orchard at dawn. (past)

**8.** They had <u>rise</u> in the dark for a cold breakfast. (past participle)

**9.** The farmer <u>learn</u> about cross pollination. (past)

**10.** She has <u>lay</u> the warming pots around the trees. (past participle)

**11.** Mr. Charles <u>teach</u> us about hummingbirds. (past)

**12.** The hummingbirds have <u>leave</u> for their summer grounds. (past participle)

**13.** A hummingbird almost never <u>sit</u> still on a branch. (present)

**14.** <u>Lay</u> the binoculars near that window. (present)

Write the verb that correctly completes each sentence.

**15.** They (sat, set) in the back of the pickup truck.

**16.** Someone (had risen, had raised) the tarp for them.

**17.** One worker (learned, taught) the others a folk song.

**18.** Each man (learned, taught) a different part.

**19.** Little Ben (lay, laid) down on his father's lap.

**20.** His father (leave, let) him sleep for a while.

**21.** Enrique (borrowed, lent) the boy a jacket for a pillow.

**22.** The rain stopped, and mist (rose, raised) from the ground.

# Know Your Audience

When you write, you need to **know your audience.**
This means that you keep in mind who is going to read
your writing. Your tone, word choice, and subject should
be suited to your audience.

**Friend as Audience**   This story is awesome!

**Teacher as Audience**   The story *Juan Verdades* is
well written.

 Match each sentence with the audience for which it seems
best suited.

| | | |
|---|---|---|
| best friend | school principal | teammates |
| kindergartners | older sister | your teacher |

**1.** Listen up! If it rains, leave the equipment and go inside the
locker room.

**2.** That's so cool!

**3.** We would like to suggest two new policies for school field trips.

**4.** We all agreed to have a class party next week, if that's all right
with you.

**5.** Who can tell me which is the letter *A*?

**6.** Mom said you have to let me go with you.

 Choose an audience from the box above and
write an e-mail note to that audience. Include
a greeting and at least two sentences.

# E-Mail

> An **e-mail** is an electronic letter (usually a brief, friendly message) sent by computer. Because it is frequently informal, e-mail communication provides special opportunities to convey your voice and feelings. However, you should still use correct grammar, spelling, and punctuation.

From: holly @ averschoolk12.edu

To: mward @ averschoolk12.edu

Subject: Juan Verdades

Dear Mr. Ward,

You asked us to write you an e-mail with our opinions about *Juan Verdades*. The story was all right, but I don't think kids can relate to this folk tale.

First of all, it's not very realistic. I just don't think there's such a thing as a person who "can't lie." No way! I don't think you could find one person in the world who hasn't told a lie. Not even Gandhi!

A bigger problem is the story's moral—if you always tell the truth, good things will happen to you. Juan Verdades stole apples and then confessed. And what was his punishment? He got a ranch and a beautiful wife! Come on! I confessed when I accidentally broke my mom's bracelet. All I got was a week's grounding for borrowing it without permission.

So, Mr. Ward, I don't think the story was a useful one. We need to read stories that are more like real life.

Holly Bannerman

**Intentional fragments are appropriate for an e-mail.**

**Writer uses details to support her opinion.**

**Writer uses an engaging, informal voice.**

# Prepositions

A **preposition** shows a relationship between a noun or pronoun and another word in the sentence, such as a verb, adjective, or other noun. A **prepositional phrase** begins with a **preposition** and usually ends with a noun or pronoun. The noun or pronoun is called the **object of the preposition.**

Prepositional Phrase
↓
The ambulance raced <u>to the hospital</u>.
↑            ↑
Preposition    Object of the preposition

Here are some common prepositions: *about, above, across, after, against, along, among, around, as, at, before, behind, below, beneath, beside, between, beyond, by, down, during, except, for, from, in, inside, into, near, of, off, on, onto, out, outside, over, past, since, through, throughout, to, toward, under, underneath, until, up, upon, with, within, without.*

• Like an adjective, a prepositional phrase can modify a noun or pronoun. The girl <u>in the red hat</u> is my sister.

• Like an adverb, a prepositional phrase can modify a verb. Elizabeth walked <u>into the classroom</u>.

Ⓐ Write the prepositional phrase or phrases in each sentence. Write *P* above the preposition and *O* above the object of the preposition in each prepositional phrase.

1. My friend works at a college in Philadelphia.

2. The president dismissed the meeting before lunch.

3. Eva felt discouraged about her progress in her career.

4. The medical profession was not ready for a female surgeon.

5. Elizabeth worked as a student nurse in the maternity ward.

**B**  Write the prepositional phrase in each sentence. Write *Adjective* if the phrase acts as an adjective. Write *Adverb* if it acts as an adverb.

1. Both men and women have been pioneers in medicine.
2. Women struggled for equal rights.
3. Few women worked outside the home.
4. Medical school was an impossible dream for most women.
5. A few courageous women fought against prejudice.
6. Elizabeth Blackwell became the first woman doctor in the United States.
7. This was not accomplished without a great struggle.
8. Her achievement has been remembered through the years.
9. The secret force behind her success was determination.
10. An important characteristic of any doctor is knowledge, not gender.

**C**  Add a prepositional phrase to each sentence. Write the sentence.

11. One time I got sick.
12. The teacher sent me.
13. The school nurse took my temperature.
14. Then he called my dad.
15. I lay down and waited.
16. Soon Dad picked me up.
17. The flu kept me home.
18. The doctor recommended fluids and rest.
19. I didn't enjoy my "vacation."
20. My fever, aches, and pains disappeared.

# Test Preparation

✓ Write the letter of the prepositions in each sentence.

**1.** Doctors work for long hours at clinics and hospitals.

   **A** for, hours   **C** for, at

   **B** long, at    **D** clinics, hospitals

**2.** They read about new findings and keep up with new treatments.

   **A** about, with **C** and, up

   **B** findings,   **D** read, keep treatments

**3.** At any hour of the night, they could be called.

   **A** hour, could **C** any, be

   **B** At, of     **D** of, night

**4.** A patient in trouble needs care without delay.

   **A** care, delay **C** A, in

   **B** needs, care **D** in, without

✓ Write the letter of the objects of the prepositions in each sentence.

**5.** Many doctors specialize in one kind of medicine.

   **A** doctors, medicine

   **B** specialize, in

   **C** kind, medicine

   **D** Many, one

**6.** An ophthalmologist knows about diseases of the eyes.

   **A** ophthalmologist, knows

   **B** diseases, eyes

   **C** ophthalmologist, diseases

   **D** knows, eyes

**7.** The woman with red hair is a surgeon at the clinic.

   **A** with, red

   **B** hair, surgeon

   **C** woman, clinic

   **D** hair, clinic

**8.** Rico is a resident in dermatology, or the care of the skin.

   **A** dermatology, skin

   **B** in, or

   **C** care, skin

   **D** Rico, dermatology

# Review

✓ Write the prepositional phrase or phrases in each sentence. Write *P* above the preposition and *O* above the object of the preposition in each prepositional phrase.

   1. Helen hurried down the sidewalk to the hospital.
   2. Her shift begins at 11 P.M. and lasts until 7 A.M.
   3. Many experts work in a hospital.
   4. After doctors and nurses, there is a great need for administrators, dieticians, and lab workers.
   5. The hospital is full of caring professionals.
   6. Robert works as a volunteer in the gift shop.
   7. The sixth graders brought teddy bears for the children with serious illnesses.
   8. An ambulance with flashing lights sped onto the scene.

✓ Write each prepositional phrase. Write *Adjective* if it acts as an adjective in the sentence. Write *Adverb* if it acts as an adverb.

   9. People once had strange ideas about the causes of diseases.
   10. Surgical instruments were not sterilized before surgery.
   11. Bacteria cause infections in wounds.
   12. Today surgeons scrub carefully for operations.
   13. Bacteria exist everywhere around us and even in our bodies.
   14. The immune system protects you with an army of cells.
   15. White blood cells recognize invaders and swarm to the rescue.
   16. A person with the flu has millions of white blood cells in his or her body.

# Transition Words

> **Transition words** make "bridges" between sentences, paragraphs, or ideas. Some transition words show sequence (*first, next, then, finally*). Some point out examples or evidence (*for example, that is, so*). Others signal comparisons (*and, as, like, similar, both*) or contrasts (*but, however, unlike, not, on the other hand*).

 Write the best word or words from the box to make the sentences in the paragraph below flow smoothly.

| Then | but | First |
|------|-----|-------|
| However | For example | |

    I'd like to become a doctor someday. I think it's a very rewarding profession, **(1)** ____ it's also hard work. **(2)** ____, you have to study for many years! **(3)** ____ of all, you have to get good grades in school and college. **(4)** ____ you have to go to medical school for several more years. **(5)** ____, once you get your medical degree, all the effort seems worthwhile.

 Add your own transition words to make the paragraph below clearer and easier to read. You may want to combine some sentences.

    I wanted to play hockey. Sixth-graders weren't allowed to join the league. I was big enough and fast enough to play with the older kids. I practiced more on my own. I watched the team play. They saw I was dedicated enough to play. They let me join.

="20">

WRITING MODEL

# Writing for Tests

> Write a paragraph <u>comparing and contrasting</u> <u>women's rights</u> in <u>the 1800s</u> to women's rights today. Use <u>transition words</u> and <u>details</u> to show <u>likenesses and differences</u>.

**Formal voice is appropriate for an essay.**

**Transition words signal comparisons and contrasts.**

**Facts support ideas.**

**Writer injects a personal note in the final sentence to add impact.**

### Step by Step

Women's rights have come a long way in the last hundred and fifty years, but women still have farther to go. In the 1800s, women struggled to gain basic rights that laid the foundation for women's rights today. Women also fought in different industries for higher positions. In the mid-1800s, no woman had ever gone to medical school and become a doctor. However, today women all across the country become doctors. Women broke the pattern and worked in careers that were thought to be only for men. Unlike today, women could not vote in the 1800s. Now, not only can they vote, but more women hold elective office than ever before. Women continue to break barriers in many different ways. Though there have been advances in women's rights, there is still room for improvement. For instance, no woman has ever been elected President or Vice-President. Maybe that will change in the near future—when I become President!

Writing **139**

# Subject and Object Pronouns

A personal pronoun used as the subject of a sentence is called a **subject pronoun.**

<u>He</u> published an article. <u>She</u> and <u>I</u> read the article.

A personal pronoun used as a direct object, indirect object, or object of a preposition is called an **object pronoun.**

The explorer thanked <u>them</u>. I gave the book to Becky and <u>him</u>.

- Subject pronouns are *I, you, he, she, it, we,* and *they.*
- Object pronouns are *me, you, him, her, it, us,* and *them.*
- Remember to use the correct pronoun form with a compound subject or object.
- Subject pronouns replace the nouns they represent. Do not use a subject pronoun with the noun it represents.

**No:**    Tim he went ice fishing with his brother.

**Yes:**   Tim went ice fishing with his brother.

**A** Write the correct pronoun in ( ) to complete each sentence.

**1.** Tamara and (she, her) photographed the Northern Lights.

**2.** (Them, They) took enough supplies for five years.

**3.** Curt and (she, her) will join the expedition.

**4.** The North Pole would be too cold for (I, me).

**5.** Carlos and (me, I) could lose toes.

**6.** (We, Us) know what happened to those explorers.

**7.** Seth and (he, him) are going on the class field trip.

**8.** The class accompanied (they, them) to the museum.

**9.** Mr. Jasper told Ann and (I, me) about his trip to Greenland.

**10.** He invited Ms. Eddings and (we, us) to view ancient relics.

**B** Write the pronoun in each sentence. Write *SP* if it is a subject pronoun. Write *OP* if it is an object pronoun.

1. It is a thrilling story of adventure.
2. The Arctic explorers astound my friends and me.
3. The extreme weather and danger there are scary to us.
4. Maria and I will travel by dogsled on our trip.
5. Can John and she come along for the ride?
6. The travelers took twenty pairs of dogs and tons of supplies with them.
7. Peary and they continued to the North Pole.
8. He and Henson may have reached the Pole on April 6, 1909.
9. The public finally gave him credit for being first.
10. However, because there was no firm proof, we cannot be sure.
11. The guide will let you drive the sled for a while.
12. Anika trained for months so that the team would obey her.

**C** Use each of the phrases below correctly in a sentence. Write the sentence.

13. the campers and them
14. he and I
15. Charlie and she
16. you and I
17. the guide and him
18. Ginny and he
19. Grace and us
20. Sean and I

# Test Preparation

Write the letter of the pronoun that correctly replaces the underlined word or words in each sentence.

1. <u>Lewis and Clark</u> explored the Louisiana Purchase.

   **A** Them    **C** Us
   **B** They    **D** We

2. They were sent by <u>President Thomas Jefferson</u>.

   **A** them    **C** him
   **B** he    **D** it

3. <u>The Louisiana Purchase</u> had just been acquired.

   **A** It    **C** They
   **B** He    **D** Them

4. Jefferson chose <u>Meriwether Lewis</u> as commander.

   **A** you    **C** he
   **B** she    **D** him

5. <u>Lewis</u> asked William Clark to join him.

   **A** He    **C** Him
   **B** She    **D** Her

6. The expedition might not have succeeded without <u>Sacajawea</u>.

   **A** they    **C** her
   **B** she    **D** he

7. <u>The horses</u> carried the men and supplies long distances.

   **A** Us    **C** Him
   **B** They    **D** Her

8. When <u>the river</u> ended, they made their way on foot.

   **A** us    **C** it
   **B** he    **D** her

9. <u>Jim and I</u> studied this famous expedition.

   **A** Us    **C** They
   **B** We    **D** Them

10. Will Ms. Underwood help <u>Jim and me</u> with our report?

    **A** he    **C** we
    **B** I    **D** us

# Review

✓ Write *SP* if the underlined word is a subject pronoun.
Write *OP* if the word is an object pronoun.

1. The travelers explored much of the upper Midwest and Northwest, and <u>they</u> met many Native Americans.

2. Usually the natives gave <u>them</u> food and assistance.

3. Sacajawea spoke some of the native languages, so <u>she</u> helped smooth the way.

4. Lewis kept a journal and filled <u>it</u> with his observations and sketches of new landforms, plants, and animals.

5. Every man on the expedition noted the wonders around <u>him</u>.

6. Lewis and <u>they</u> were seeing some sights for the first time.

7. All of the trip was difficult, but the worst part of <u>it</u> was the mountain crossing.

8. <u>I</u> think that Lewis would have written a fantastic book about the adventure.

9. His early death deprived <u>us</u> of this work about the expedition.

10. <u>We</u> must relive Lewis and Clark's adventure in our imaginations.

✓ Write the correct pronoun or pronouns in ( ) to complete each sentence.

11. Are there any new frontiers for (us, we) to explore?

12. The ocean floor is vast, and much of (it, they) is unexplored.

13. Jacques Cousteau was an ocean pioneer. (He, Him) brought wonders of the deep onto our TV screens.

14. Ginny and (I, me) think we would like to deep-sea dive.

15. Dad asked if (he, him) could rent scuba gear at the marina.

16. Mom said scuba diving doesn't interest (her, she).

# Answer the 5 Ws and How

A news story gives key information about an event. It answers a set of questions called the **5 Ws and How:** *Who? What? Where? When? Why? How?* This essential information tells readers about an event in direct, concrete, and objective sentences.

Some dogs got away the other day.
(Answers only *Who* and *What*)

Two sled dogs escaped from Neil Olafsen's yard yesterday afternoon. Olafsen said they got out by digging under the walls of their pen.
(Answers all six questions)

 Choose the news story lead that best answers the 5 Ws and How. Explain why your choice is the best and why the other two are not.

1. Three inches of snow fell yesterday. They had trouble plowing it all, but finally it melted. There's no cause for alarm. Things were back to normal today.

2. A man and a woman were found stranded on frozen Reindeer Lake yesterday, due to an ill-advised skating adventure during a blizzard. Marion and Geoffrey Harden of Antlerville, Vermont, were a little cold but not seriously injured.

3. The Prime Minister of Norway was there last Wednesday, as were several Olympic cross-country ski champions. The Oslo Banquet Hall was completely redecorated for the festivities.

 Choose one of the story leads above that was incomplete. Rewrite the lead, adding details to answer the 5 Ws and How.

# News Story

When you want to know what's happening in your community or around the world, odds are you can find out in a **news story.** A news story puts the most important information in a lead sentence. Details are provided in later sentences.

Headline gets reader's attention.

Lead sentence gives most important information.

Details are given later.

## Bold Norwegian First to Ski Across Greenland

July 20, 1888—A young Norwegian scientist, Fridtjof Nansen, became the first person ever to cross Greenland on skis yesterday. A careful planner and accomplished athlete, Nansen, 26, was dropped off with his party on the uninhabited eastern coast of the world's largest island. Taking advantage of Inuit survival methods, Nansen and his five companions used dog sledges, kayaks, and snow houses as they forged their way west toward civilization. In a bold move, Nansen's group packed only enough supplies for a one-way trip. They knew that they would either succeed or die trying. The Greenland ski trip was Nansen's first expedition. The young outdoorsman and poet says he is planning future expeditions.

# Pronouns and Antecedents

A **pronoun** takes the place of a noun or nouns. An **antecedent,** or referent, is the noun or nouns to which the pronoun refers. A pronoun and its antecedent must agree in number and gender.

Before you use a pronoun, ask yourself whether the antecedent is singular or plural. If the antecedent is singular, decide whether it is masculine, feminine, or neuter. Then choose a pronoun that agrees. In the following sentences, the antecedents are underlined once; the pronouns are underlined twice.

Sal and Jo bought a book, and they read it together.

Erik brought a camera so he could take pictures.

**A** Write the pronoun that refers to the underlined antecedent.

1. Jane Goodall observed chimpanzees and helped them survive.
2. Chimpanzees have interesting ways of finding food when they are hungry.
3. Although Vicky learned to say four words, very few people could understand her.
4. The class was excited when we got a letter from Jane Goodall.
5. Ai grabbed the doll and hugged it tightly.
6. In 1961, Ham was placed aboard a rocket to see whether he could survive the space flight.
7. Paige and I wanted to hold the baby chimp, but the mother would not let us.
8. After Lucy grabbed a stone, she used it to crack open a nut.

**B** Write the antecedent in each item. Then write the pronoun in ( ) that matches the antecedent.

1. Chimpanzees have brains much like human brains, and (it, they) behave like humans in some ways.

2. A chimpanzee will pick up a stick and use (it, he) as a tool.

3. Lucy learned sign language and made up signs for objects whose names (it, she) did not know.

4. Ham was a male chimpanzee who went into space in 1961. Although frightened, (he, them) survived.

5. Barb and I thought the baby chimps were imitating (us, we).

6. Baby chimps cling to their mothers but are sometimes taken from (her, them).

7. Does the zoo treat chimpanzees well? (It, They) has living quarters with a natural habitat.

8. The chimpanzees live in family groups that give (them, it) nearly normal lives.

**C** Read each sentence. Write another sentence with a pronoun that refers to the underlined words.

9. Many chimpanzees have been taught American Sign Language.

10. Jane Goodall has worked with and studied chimpanzees all her adult life.

11. A male chimpanzee and a female chimpanzee are roughly the same height.

12. The wilderness homes of chimpanzees are threatened.

13. Jane Goodall addressed the children of our school.

14. All people must make an effort to solve this problem.

15. Think of some things you can do to help preserve habitats.

# Test Preparation

✓ Write the letter of the pronoun that correctly completes each sentence.

1. Did you watch the monkeys? Are ____ like people?

   A you       C her
   B him       D they

2. I watched the mother with her baby. ____ taught it to hunt termites.

   A Her       C We
   B She       D It

3. The monkeys ate bananas that the keeper had given ____.

   A them      C it
   B he        D I

4. Our class visited the zoo, and ____ had a great time.

   A me        C us
   B we        D them

5. We learned about members of the ape family. ____ come in all different sizes.

   A It        C Them
   B You       D They

6. Jane Goodall knows about chimpanzees because ____ has observed them for decades.

   A he        C I
   B she       D us

7. Chimpanzees may know they are related to people because they communicate with ____.

   A her       C us
   B they      D it

8. The teacher told her students, "____ also need to observe the orangutans and gorillas."

   A Them      C He
   B It        D You

9. I took pictures of the baby chimpanzees to school with ____.

   A me        C they
   B she       D we

10. Jodi and I want to become zoologists. ____ will travel to Africa to study animals.

    A Her      C We
    B Them     D Him

# Review

 Write each sentence. Circle the pronoun and underline its antecedent.

1. Mr. Smith asked Roy to help him set up the display.
2. The class watched a movie about chimpanzees after studying about them.
3. Chimpanzees resemble people, right down to having facial expressions like us.
4. The chimpanzee's eyes were large and brown. They seemed sad and wise.
5. The big cats at the zoo closed their eyes and ignored the activity around them.
6. The lion has a keen sense of smell, which helps it hunt.
7. The giraffes seemed content in their enclosure because it was large and forested.
8. The alligators and crocodiles lay in the sunshine, which they seemed to enjoy.
9. Dr. Benchley looked closely at slides she had taken in Africa.
10. Aaron wanted to take one of the stuffed animals with him.

 Write the pronoun that agrees with the antecedent. Then write the antecedent to which the pronoun refers.

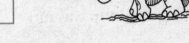

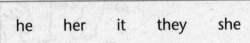

| he | her | it | they | she |

11. Mary Alice asked Tom to get a ticket for ___ .
12. The circus had come to town, and ___ looked exciting.
13. A man rode on an elephant's back. ___ held a pet monkey.
14. A girl put on quite a show. ___ danced and leaped around the ring.
15. The acrobats soared above the crowd. ___ made everyone gasp with their daring.

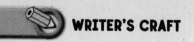

# Use Vivid Words

**Vivid words** create a sharp picture in the reader's mind. Replace vague words with vivid adjectives, nouns, and verbs to make your writing sparkle!

**Vague**  An animal went into the box.

**Vivid**  The sprightly chimp scampered into the rickety cardboard box.

Replace the underlined word in each sentence with a more vivid or exact word. You can also replace other words or add more vivid words. Write the new sentences.

1. We <u>went</u> to the ape exhibit.
2. Their habitat looked <u>nice</u>.
3. The keeper <u>said</u> something to her assistant.
4. We saw the <u>animals</u> eat lunch.
5. They like <u>fruit</u>.
6. One <u>ate</u> all its food.
7. A male ape <u>was</u> in a hammock.
8. Two baby apes <u>played</u> on his stomach.
9. They <u>made</u> a lot of noise.
10. Our field trip was <u>fun</u>.

Write a description of an animal. Use vivid words to describe what the animal looks and acts like.

# Story About an Animal

A **story** can tell about an event or how characters solve a problem. It has a beginning, middle, and end. To make a story interesting, writers use devices such as suspense, conflict, dialogue, and humor.

**A Llama's Laugh**

Conflict and tension get the story rolling.

Lloyd, the llama, was worried. He had to improve his mountain delivery service, or he'd lose his most important customer—Monica, the spider monkey.

Lloyd hauled heavy packages across the steep, cold mountains for smaller animals. The alpacas had been enticing customers away from Lloyd's service. Just yesterday, Monica had said, "Look, Lloyd, I like you. But the alpacas are always on time, and you've been late." Lloyd knew this was his last chance.

Suspense propels the reader to the conclusion.

He was wondering where he would go for lunch when the phone rang ominously. Al, the alpaca, was calling! "I hear Monica has given you one last chance," bellowed Al. "Slip up and the monkey's business is mine!" Lloyd grunted and hung up.

Humor ends the story on an upbeat note.

"Forget lunch," Lloyd muttered. "Instead of going out, I'll pack a lunch." Suddenly, Lloyd burst into shrieks and honks of llama laughter. "Get it?" he yelled to no one in particular. "'Alpaca' lunch! I crack myself up sometimes." Now Lloyd was ready for the challenge.

# Possessive Pronouns

Pronouns that show ownership are called **possessive pronouns.** A possessive pronoun and its antecedent must agree in number and gender. Before you use a possessive pronoun, ask yourself whether the antecedent is singular or plural. If the antecedent is singular, decide whether it is masculine, feminine, or neuter. Then choose a pronoun that agrees.

**Possessive Pronouns**

*My/mine, your/yours, his, her/hers, its, our/ours, their/theirs*

- *My, your, her, our,* and *their* are always used with nouns.
  Your understanding of history is important.

- *Mine, yours, hers, ours,* and *theirs* stand alone.
  Is that history book yours?

- *His* and *its* can be used with nouns or can stand alone.
  His report was on a biography of Satchel Paige.
  The book about Satchel Paige was his.

- Do not use an apostrophe with a possessive pronoun.

**A** Write the possessive pronouns in the sentences.

1. Homesteaders built their houses by piling layers of sod.
2. The Nicodemus Blues was one of our nation's first black baseball teams.
3. That Louisiana farmer was able to buy his own land.
4. The Union Army soldiers knew the uniforms were theirs.
5. The report about African American cowboys is mine.
6. My dream of freedom is the same as yours.

**B** Write the pronoun in ( ) that correctly completes each sentence.

1. African Americans served (their, his) country in the Civil War.
2. The Tenth Cavalry had only black soldiers in (its, our) ranks.
3. The black soldier was given poor equipment and weapons to protect (his, their) life.
4. Because these soldiers fought bravely, honor was (yours, theirs).
5. The Wild West is a part of (our, ours) cultural heritage.
6. Is this book about African Americans in the West (mine, my) or (your, yours)?
7. The American West had (its, their) racial troubles, but it also offered opportunity.
8. (Her, Hers) report on the Buffalo Soldiers was interesting, but (your, yours) was better.
9. David did (their, his) report on the Civil War years, and we did (our, ours) on the years after the war.
10. We will remember these soldiers and (his, their) contributions to (our, its) history.

**C** Replace each underlined word or phrase with a possessive pronoun. Write the sentences.

11. For homesteaders, life was lonely, and homesteaders' work was endless.
12. Today we Americans enjoy many luxuries in Americans' lives.
13. The Home Place is a restored homestead brought to life by actors who work in the Home Place's buildings and fields.
14. The sixth graders visited there as part of the sixth graders' spring field trip.
15. Ms. Isak was in charge of the field trip, and the plan to go to Home Place was Ms. Isak's plan.

# Test Preparation

Write the letter of the pronoun that correctly completes each sentence.

1. Hollywood has ____ own version of the West.

   A  they     C  their
   B  its      D  our

2. John Wayne gave ____ own style to the cowboy hero.

   A  her      C  his
   B  their    D  my

3. Are black cowboys part of ____ idea of the West?

   A  your     C  ours
   B  mine     D  theirs

4. Black cowboys played ____ part in taming the West.

   A  my       C  theirs
   B  its      D  their

5. Calamity Jane made ____ mark on the American imagination.

   A  our      C  her
   B  mine     D  hers

6. Early settlers of the West are ____ heroes.

   A  mine     C  hers
   B  they     D  our

7. Is this movie ____ or his?

   A  our      C  my
   B  hers     D  her

8. The movie *High Noon* is ____ favorite western.

   A  my       C  ours
   B  theirs   D  hers

9. Most of ____ notions about the West are romantic.

   A  our      C  theirs
   B  hers     D  yours

10. History tells ____ own, less romantic story.

    A  ours     C  its
    B  his      D  their

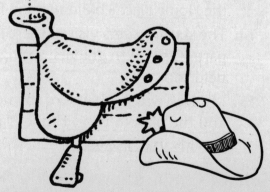

# Review

✓ Write the possessive pronoun in each sentence.

1. A long ride on a horse is my idea of a good time.
2. Cowboys rode their horses for days on end.
3. A horse was a cowboy's friend, and its care was important.
4. A cowboy often slept outdoors with his saddle for a pillow.
5. My family stayed at a dude ranch for our vacation.
6. The trail guide shared her knowledge about the West.
7. The fancy bridle and saddle are hers.
8. Our bunk beds were quite comfortable.
9. The top bunk by the door was mine.
10. The scrapbook you are holding is ours.

✓ Write the pronoun that correctly completes each sentence.

11. Will you travel by wagon train on (its, your) trip?
12. Join (our, ours) week-long expedition out West!
13. All travelers must bring (his, their) own bedrolls.
14. Each team of mules has (their, its) own character.
15. Jenny is stubborn, but (her, his) personality is sweet.
16. Max pulls hard, but he thinks the lead should be (his, their).
17. The campfires are lit, and (their, theirs) light is comforting in the darkness.
18. Are you making coffee over (mine, your) fire?
19. Max made the flapjacks, so the first ones are (his, my).
20. The dust stung (hers, my) eyes as we rode.
21. When I get home, the first shower will be (our, mine).
22. The red suitcases with black handles are (your, ours).

# Order

You may describe a setting, event, or character using many details. Arranging these details in an **order** can make your writing easier to read. You can list details in spatial order—left to right, front to back, top to bottom. You can list things in order of importance. Events can be written in time order.

**Spatial Order**

I see a horse on the left, a cow in the middle, and a chicken on the right.

**Order of Importance**

Her sprightly walk surprised me, and her twinkling eyes delighted me. However, her outrageous purple hat tickled me most of all.

**Time Order**

The bell rang, books snapped shut, and students poured into the hall.

 Write *Yes* if the items in each list are arranged in order. If they are not, write the items in order. Write which type of order is used in each list.

   **1.** train engine, caboose, box car
   **2.** President, Vice-President, Governor
   **3.** summer, spring, winter, fall
   **4.** head, shoulders, knees, toes
   **5.** wake up, get dressed, eat breakfast, go to school

 Describe something you see. Write a paragraph that tells the details in spatial order, order of importance, or time order.

# Describe a Setting

**Setting** is the time and place in which a story occurs, such as a frontier home in the 1870s. A setting provides a background for a story and can reveal information about the characters and events.

**Once Upon a Time on the Plains**

Setting includes both place and time.

Our story takes place in a log cabin in the late 1800s. The cabin, built by Jedediah and Earline Whitley, sits on a low-rising hill surrounded by tall grasses and plowed land. Behind the cabin is a shed. A broken plowshare by the shed shows how hard it has been to "bust" the sod.

Vivid details give a sense of mood.

As night begins to fall, a kerosene lamp shines through the cracks in the plank door. The door is the only opening in the windowless cabin.

Details of setting are presented in spatial order.

On the left side of the room stand one bed for the parents and one for the two daughters. In the middle of the room are a handmade table and four chairs. On the right side of the room, a hearth with a blazing fire throws off heat.

A single framed drawing decorates the wall of the cabin. This picture shows Jed and Earline when they were much younger and still enslaved.

# Indefinite and Reflexive Pronouns

**Indefinite pronouns** may not refer to specific words. They do not always have definite antecedents: <u>No one</u> got a new uniform.

Some common indefinite pronouns are listed below:

| **Singular Indefinite Pronouns** | **Plural Indefinite Pronouns** |
|---|---|
| someone, somebody, anyone, anybody, everyone, everybody, something, no one, either, each | few, several, both, others, many, all, some |

- Use singular verb forms with singular indefinite pronouns and plural verb forms with plural indefinite pronouns: <u>Everyone</u> wants to go into space. <u>Few</u> get the chance.

**Reflexive pronouns** reflect the action of the verb back on the subject. Reflexive pronouns end in *-self* or *-selves*:
The cadet imagined <u>herself</u> a hero.

| **Singular Reflexive Pronouns** | **Plural Reflexive Pronouns** |
|---|---|
| myself, yourself, himself, herself, itself | ourselves, yourselves, themselves |

- There are no such words as *hisself, theirself, theirselves,* or *ourself.*

**A** Write the indefinite or reflexive pronoun in each sentence. Identify the pronoun as *indefinite* or *reflexive* and *singular* or *plural*.

1. Few wonder where the captain is heading.
2. I asked myself why I had become a cadet.
3. Each of the cadets knows the way to the space port.
4. We transmitted the data ourselves.
5. Everyone in the class writes a report.

**B** Write the correct pronoun in ( ) to complete each sentence.

1. (Everybody, Some) believe that we will find life on other planets.

2. The sun (itself, himself) could not harbor life.

3. (Few, Somebody) know about the vast number of galaxies in the universe.

4. (Someone, Several) in the back row is speaking.

5. People are kidding (theirselves, themselves) if they think there is no other life out there.

6. (All, Each) of the galaxies are bound to contain at least one planet with conditions like those on Earth.

7. Does (anybody, others) think Mars or Venus has life?

8. (Both, Either) of these planets are close to Earth.

9. (Each, Others) in our solar system are too close or too far from the sun.

10. I thought to (myself, yourselves), "I'll believe it when I see it."

**C** Write a sentence using the indefinite pronoun and the correct verb in ( ).

11. something (seem, seems)

12. all (is, are)

13. few (want, wants)

14. no one (understand, understands)

15. (do, does) anyone remember

# Test Preparation

✓ Write the letter of the correct pronoun(s) to complete each sentence.

1. Will you and he go to the play by ____?

   A hisself
   B himself
   C yourself
   D yourselves

2. ____ have dressed as space cadets.

   A Several
   B Somebody
   C No one
   D Yourself

3. Mary thinks of ____ as the best actress of all.

   A anything
   B yourselves
   C herself
   D themselves

4. ____ has any ideas about the space scenes.

   A Ourselves
   B Both
   C Some
   D No one

5. ____ wants a black backdrop with a few stars.

   A Everyone
   B Several
   C Myself
   D Hisself

6. If ____ of us work an hour or so, we can finish the job.

   A everyone
   B all
   C each
   D anyone

7. ____ has painted that wall by ____.

   A Many, theirself
   B No one, themselves
   C Someone, himself or herself
   D You, yourselves

8. ____ of you deserve a hand because you outdid ____.

   A Some, themselves
   B Both, yourselves
   C Everyone, itself
   D No one, yourself

# Review

✓ Write the indefinite or reflexive pronoun in each sentence.
Identify the pronoun as *indefinite* or *reflexive* and *singular* or *plural*.

1. Many of the cadets laugh during the humorous performance.

2. Cadets give themselves enough time to dress every morning.

3. I struggle to understand the computer system while others learn it right away.

4. The officer usually does the paperwork herself.

5. Everyone stands on the bridge of the spacecraft waiting for liftoff and departure.

6. A spaceship can be set to fly itself.

7. The engineer leaves the hatch open until all have departed.

8. You will have to cook the Voloreain space slugs yourself.

✓ Write the correct pronoun in ( ) to complete each sentence.

9. (Many, Everyone) has dreamed about space travel.

10. (Few, Someone) get the chance to do it.

11. Astronauts train (himself, themselves) to live in zero gravity.

12. We told (ourselves, yourselves) we wouldn't feel the effects.

13. After months in space, (everybody, some) lose muscle mass.

14. Has (anyone, all) measured space travelers' heights before and after their trips?

15. The body can adjust (himself, itself) to changes in atmosphere.

16. Astronauts face dangers, but (each, few) is glad for the chance to travel in space.

17. Anne pushed (herself, yourself) physically and emotionally at space camp.

18. I (himself, myself) wouldn't apply for the space program.

# Stage Directions

**Stage directions** can set a scene, describe an action, or tell a character's state of mind. Because plays, shows, and movies happen in "real time," stage directions are written in the present tense. They are set in italics or underlined and enclosed in parentheses.

**Examples**

*(The scene: A suburban kitchen that has a sink full of dishes.)* (Sets the scene)

*(He moves slowly toward the door.)* (Describes an action)

**HENRY** *(slyly)*: (Tells character's state of mind)

 Write the purpose of each of the following stage directions: *sets the scene, describes an action,* or *tells character's state of mind.*

1. *(He picks up the envelope.)*

2. *(suspicious):*

3. *(The lights fade. It is night.)*

4. *(two hours later in the garden)*

5. *(Suddenly, two llamas enter the room.)*

6. *(He speaks quietly.):*

7. *(impatiently):*

8. *(Bedroom is strewn with toys.)*

 Using only stage directions, write a four-sentence "play." Set the scene and describe the characters' actions.

# TV Script

A **TV script,** or play written to be performed on television, is similar to a story. It has characters, plot, setting, and dialogue. A TV script is also similar to a play. It has stage directions.

Script begins with title, characters, and setting.

### O'Brien's Dilemma

*adapted from* Mother Fletcher's Gift

**CHARACTERS:**

Officer O'Brien, a New York City police officer

Mother Fletcher

**SETTING**: *(Interior: A small but spotless bedroom. O'BRIEN is standing by a bed. MOTHER FLETCHER is sitting upright in the bed, looking stern.)*

**O'BRIEN:** *(getting out his pad):* What's your name, please?

Dialogue reveals character traits.

**MOTHER FLETCHER:** I'm Mother Fletcher. Now are you going to get me an ambulance?

**O'BRIEN:** We can't call an ambulance for just anyone.

**MOTHER FLETCHER:** Look here! I am not just anyone. I am Mother Fletcher. Use that radio of yours.

*(O'BRIEN flips out his radio and calls dispatch.)*

Stage directions help with mood and action.

**O'BRIEN:** All right, Ma'am. *(to radio)* Dispatch, I have a 519 here at 221 145th Street, requesting an ambulance. Subject is—*(to MOTHER FLETCHER)* What is your age?

**MOTHER FLETCHER:** *(glaring at him):* Full grown.

*(Fade to black)*

**LESSON 20**

# Using *Who* and *Whom*

The pronoun **who** is used as a subject of a sentence or clause.

Who called me? (*Who* is the subject of the sentence.)

My brother asked <u>who</u> had called me. (*Who* is the subject of the dependent clause *who had called me*.)

The pronoun **whom** is used as the object of a preposition or as a direct object.

To <u>whom</u> did you give the assignment? (*Whom* is the object of the preposition *to*.)

This was an assistant <u>whom</u> he trusted. (*Whom* is the direct object of the verb *trusted* in the dependent clause *whom he trusted*.)

<u>Whom</u> did you see? (*Whom* is a direct object.)

You can check if *whom* should be used as a direct object. Change the word order so that the subject comes first. (*Whom* did you see? You did see *whom?*)

**A** Write the pronoun in ( ) that correctly completes each sentence.

**1.** (Who, Whom) invested in Edison Electric Light Company?

**2.** With (who, whom) did Edison test ideas for an invention?

**3.** (Who, Whom) gave us the most valuable inventions?

**4.** The committee decided on (who, whom) they would award the Nobel Prize.

**5.** The helper (who, whom) worked hardest became the top assistant.

**6.** The scientist (who, whom) you met made a wonderful discovery.

**B** Write *who* or *whom* to complete each sentence correctly. Then write *subject, object of preposition,* or *direct object* to identify how the word is used in the sentence.

1. To ____ shall we award the honor "Greatest Inventor"?
2. ____ did more than Thomas Edison?
3. Edison's workers admired "the old man," ____ worked harder and longer than anyone.
4. The person for ____ Edison worked was the consumer.
5. Someone ____ sees a use for a product will buy it.
6. ____ did you choose for your report?
7. Charles Batchelor, ____ was a machinist, became Edison's right-hand man and close friend.
8. Visitors ____ visited Edison's lab in December 1879 could not believe their eyes.
9. ____ believed electricity could be used to light the darkness?
10. This genius, for ____ no task seemed too difficult, was dubbed the Wizard of Menlo Park.
11. ____ will you discuss in your report on inventors?
12. I admire Leonardo da Vinci, ____ worked in many different fields.
13. Claire will write about Bell, to ____ we owe the telephone.

**C** Choose *who* or *whom* to complete each sentence correctly. Then write the sentence and answer or explain it with another sentence.

14. (Who, Whom) is your favorite inventor?
15. If you could go back in time, (who, whom) would you most like to meet?
16. Someone (who, whom) has original, creative ideas is ____.
17. A person (who, whom) I know well is ____.
18. If you could choose one person as your role model, (who, whom) would you choose?

# Test Preparation

**1.** To <u>whom</u> did you speak?

   **A** subject
   **B** object of preposition
   **C** direct object
   **D** noun

**2.** The person <u>who</u> answered the phone was a man.

   **A** direct object
   **B** verb
   **C** subject
   **D** object of preposition

**3.** A friend <u>whom</u> you remember well called last night.

   **A** object of preposition
   **B** adjective
   **C** direct object
   **D** subject

**4.** You are the one to <u>whom</u> she wished to speak.

   **A** verb
   **B** subject
   **C** direct object
   **D** object of preposition

✓ Write the letter of the sentence that is correct.

**5.** **A** Whom are you inviting?
   **B** With who did she attend?
   **C** He is a boss who everyone admires.
   **D** Whom said that?

**6.** **A** Whom is going with us?
   **B** Joe, whom you know, will go.
   **C** The woman who you saw will be our guide.
   **D** Everyone whom visits the museum loves it.

**7.** **A** Who invented lightning rods?
   **B** Ben Franklin is the one whom did that.
   **C** The guide tells anybody whom asks.
   **D** With who did Franklin work?

**8.** **A** Who shall we ask?
   **B** That is the person to who I gave the job.
   **C** You know who will do the best job.
   **D** For who did you vote?

# Review

 Write the pronoun in ( ) that correctly completes each sentence.

1. (Who, Whom) shall we study next?
2. Thomas Edison is the inventor for (who, whom) I am voting.
3. Inventors are people (who, whom) are curious and practical.
4. I don't know anyone (who, whom) doesn't admire inventors.
5. (Who, Whom) was the most inventive American?
6. Many people (who, whom) invented practical objects contributed to our country.
7. I'd like to thank the person (who, whom) invented the safety pin.
8. There isn't anyone for (who, whom) this invention isn't useful.
9. (Who, Whom) would you thank for inventing something?
10. The inventor of the microwave oven is someone (who, whom) I would applaud.

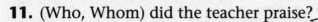

Write *who* or *whom* to complete each sentence correctly. Then write *subject, object of preposition,* or *direct object* to tell how the word is used in the sentence.

11. (Who, Whom) did the teacher praise?
12. (Who, Whom) asked that question?
13. (Who, Whom) were Dot and Dash?
14. Those were Edison's nicknames for his son and daughter, (who, whom) he loved dearly.
15. Edison is a historic figure for (who, whom) I have great admiration.
16. To (who, whom) shall I give this photograph?
17. It shows a man (who, whom) is probably Thomas Edison.
18. It also shows two children, (who, whom) must be Dot and Dash.
19. Do you recognize (who, whom) is standing in the background?
20. No, but it might be Batchelor, (who, whom) the family knew well.

# Know Your Purpose

> **Knowing your purpose** for writing helps you match *how* you write with *what* you write. It also helps you keep your writing "on track," so you don't stray from your topic. Three common purposes for writing are to entertain, to inform, and to persuade.

 Write the main purpose of each writing assignment.

> To entertain     To inform     To persuade

1. Comedy TV script
2. Recipe for making cornbread
3. Letter to voters from a candidate for mayor
4. Fairy tale
5. Instructions for using a digital camera
6. News report
7. Ad for a new shampoo
8. Story about a pet
9. Explanation of how a bird preens its feathers
10. Humorous introduction to a speech
11. Letter convincing a parent to raise your allowance
12. Short biographical sketch

 What do you know about Thomas Edison or another inventor? Use some of these facts to write a persuasive paragraph. Your purpose is to convince readers that this person is one of the world's greatest inventors.

# Writing for Tests

Write a <u>summary</u> of a biography, story, or play that you have read recently. Begin with a <u>topic sentence</u> that explains what the selection is about. Then include <u>only the most important details</u>.

**Summary starts with topic sentence.**

**Events are explained in sequence.**

**Writer uses own words or uses quotation marks if words are copied from text.**

---

### *Space Cadets:* A Summary

*Space Cadets* is a humorous play about a spaceship crew that encounters life on a new planet.

In Scene 1, we meet the Captain, First Officer, and Ensign in a spoof of TV science-fiction shows. The Captain is full of bluster, and the Ensign is eager. They and most of the crew are not very bright. Soon the ship arrives at an alien world. The Captain appoints an away team—the First Officer and two space cadets, Tom and Harold.

In Scene 2, team members arrive on the planet's surface, where they try to talk to a "space cow." They ignore Mog and Og, two aliens who look "like space dogs." Eventually, the humans get scared and dash back to their ship. Og and Mog, who turn out to be intelligent life forms, are left behind, saying, "There is no intelligent life out there."

# Contractions and Negatives

A **contraction** is a shortened form of two words. An **apostrophe** is used to show where one or more letters have been left out. Some contractions are made by combining pronouns and verbs: *we + have = we've*. Other contractions are formed by joining a verb and *not* or *have: should + not = shouldn't; could + have = could've*.

- *Won't* and *can't* are formed in special ways *(can + not = can't; will + not = won't)*.

**Negatives** are words that mean "no" or "not": *no, not, never, none, nothing*. Contractions with *n't* are negatives too. To make a negative statement, use only one negative word.

| | |
|---|---|
| **No** | Don't never use the wrong zip code. |
| **Yes** | Don't ever use the wrong zip code. |

- Use positive words, not negatives, in a sentence with *not*.

| Negative | Positive | Negative | Positive |
|---|---|---|---|
| nobody | anybody, somebody | nothing | anything, something |
| no one | anyone, someone | nowhere | anywhere, somewhere |
| none | any, all, some | never | ever, always |

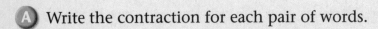

**A** Write the contraction for each pair of words.

| | | |
|---|---|---|
| **1.** they are | **3.** should not | **5.** we will |
| **2.** I have | **4.** he is | **6.** will not |

Write the word in ( ) that correctly completes each sentence.

**7.** Nothing should (ever, never) go wrong at a wedding.

**8.** The groom wasn't (nowhere, anywhere) to be found.

**B** Write the contraction in each sentence. Then write the two words used to form the contraction.

1. Martha wished she'd planned a smaller wedding.

2. Didn't you think the flowers were beautiful?

3. Ben and I would've arrived earlier if possible.

4. The bride and groom look as though they're happy.

5. When do you think they'll serve the cake?

6. You'd be amazed at how expensive a wedding can be.

7. Who's got the rings?

8. That's the most beautiful wedding gown ever!

9. Judy can't wait for the bride to throw her bouquet.

10. The band wouldn't play until after dinner.

**C** Rewrite each sentence to make it a negative sentence. Change the underlined word to a negative word or a contraction.

**Example**   <u>Everybody</u> thought the wedding was too long.
**Answer**   Nobody thought the wedding was too long.
**Example**   <u>Did</u> you take any pictures at the ceremony?
**Answer**   Didn't you take any pictures at the ceremony?

11. <u>Some</u> of the guests cried during the ceremony.

12. Has <u>anyone</u> passed out the little packages of birdseed?

13. The guests <u>will</u> throw seeds at the departing couple.

14. The seeds <u>do</u> remain on the concrete because birds eat them.

15. The couple <u>has</u> decided on a honeymoon site.

16. Almost <u>everyone</u> thinks the couple should go to Puerto Rico.

# Test Preparation

✓ Write the letter of the item that correctly completes each sentence.

1. It _____ if we leave early.

   A   doesn't hurt no one
   B   don't hurt no one
   C   doesn't hurt anyone
   D   doesnt hurt anyone

2. _____ walk with the groom?

   A   Doesn't someone never
   B   Doesn't someone ever
   C   Don't no one ever
   D   Does'nt anyone ever

3. The taller bridesmaids _____.

   A   didn't wear any heels
   B   didnt wear heels
   C   didn't wear no heels
   D   wasn't wearing no heels

4. The bride's grandparents _____.

   A   didn't never sit out a dance
   B   didnt sit out no dance
   C   didn't sit out no dance
   D   didn't sit out a dance

5. I _____ prettier shade of green.

   A   haven't never seen a
   B   haven't ever seen a
   C   havent ever seen a
   D   haven't ever seen no

6. They _____ make a toast before.

   A   hadn't never watched anyone
   B   hadn't ever watched no one
   C   hadn't ever watched anyone
   D   hadnt' ever watched anyone

7. _____ take a baby to a wedding.

   A   Nobody should ever
   B   Nobody shouldn't ever
   C   Nobody should never
   D   Nobody should not

8. I _____ like that violin solo.

   A   had never heard nothing
   B   hadn't ever heard nothing
   C   had never heard anything
   D   hadnt' ever heard anything

# Review

✓ Write the contractions for the underlined words in the sentences.

1. <u>They are</u> getting married in a month.
2. The invitations <u>have not</u> been sent yet.
3. <u>They will</u> be addressed by a calligrapher.
4. The groom <u>will not</u> forget to rent his tuxedo.
5. The church is quaint, and <u>it is</u> perfect for a small wedding.
6. The groom's best friend said <u>he would</u> be the best man.
7. The day <u>could not</u> be more beautiful.
8. The bride <u>cannot</u> remember where she put the corsages.
9. Hannah <u>did not</u> sign the guest book yet.
10. If you <u>do not</u> hurry, <u>we are</u> going to be late.

✓ Write the word in ( ) that correctly completes each sentence.

11. They couldn't find the photographer (anywhere, nowhere).
12. The planner isn't leaving (nothing, anything) to chance.
13. The soloist hasn't (ever, never) sung at a wedding.
14. No one (was, wasn't) going to leave until the bride and groom drove away.
15. Didn't (anyone, no one) make a "Just Married" sign for the car?
16. None of the guests (could, couldn't) believe how perfect everything looked.
17. The ice sculpture couldn't have been (no more, more) intricate.
18. Rob doesn't think he'll (ever, never) get married.
19. Can't (nobody, anybody) plan a truly simple wedding?
20. There isn't (no, an) answer to that question.

# Sensory Details

**Sensory details** appeal to the reader's senses—sight, hearing, smell, taste, and touch. By using these details, writers help readers visualize the characters, places, and events in a piece of writing.

| | |
|---|---|
| **Sight** | sunburned nose, blue eyes |
| **Hearing** | soft whisper, roar of a crowd |
| **Smell** | odor of fresh-baked cookies, sweaty locker room |
| **Taste** | sour lemon, spicy burrito |
| **Touch** | rough bark, slippery mud |

 Write the sense to which each sentence mainly appeals.

| sight | hearing | smell | taste | touch |
|---|---|---|---|---|

1. The rusted-out blue car was covered with dried mud.
2. A searing pain shot up my arm when I tried to move it.
3. Birds chirped cheerfully after the storm.
4. The frosting was creamy, sweet, and rich.
5. Roses filled the air with their scent.
6. The flower girl looked like an angel in her lilac dress.
7. Majestic strains of the wedding march filled the church.
8. The child's face was hot and sticky.

 Write four sentences about attending a wedding reception. Appeal to at least four of the reader's senses.

# Literary Review

> The writer of a **literary review** describes a work's strengths and weaknesses. A review also gives information about the work (but not a plot summary) to potential readers.

**The View from Saturday: A Review**

*The View from Saturday* by E. L. Konigsburg is about a boy writing a "B & B letter" to his grandparents. A "B & B letter," Noah explains, "is a bread and butter letter you write to people to thank them for having you as a houseguest."

Noah doesn't want to write the letter. However, as he thinks back on his vacation, he realizes that he had an exciting time and that writing a B & B letter is the least he could do.

The story is indeed funny. Noah takes the reader along as he recalls his fun-filled vacation. His recollections of the wedding made me laugh out loud.

Noah often calls a recollection a "Fact," as in "Fact: The cake was beautiful." This adds an unusual rhythm to the story. *The View from Saturday* is recommended reading for anyone who wants a good laugh.

Author's words are placed in quotation marks.

Writer provides information about main character.

Writer expresses opinion and supports it with facts and examples.

# Adjectives and Articles

An **adjective** describes a noun or pronoun. It tells what kind, how many, or which one.

**What Kind**  The sun shone on the <u>white</u> sand.
The wind was <u>warm</u>.

**How Many**  <u>Several</u> workers rested.
<u>One</u> man read a newspaper.

**Which One**  César lives in <u>that</u> house.
<u>Those</u> houses belong to the landowner.

The **articles** *a, an,* and *the* appear before nouns or other adjectives. Use *a* before a word that begins with a consonant sound. Use *an* before a word that begins with a vowel sound. Use *the* before words beginning with any letter.

He spent <u>a</u> long day pulling beets out of <u>the</u> ground.
It was <u>an</u> awful job.

A **proper adjective** is formed from a proper noun. Proper adjectives are always capitalized.

César Chávez is an <u>American</u> hero.

**A** Write each sentence. Underline adjectives once and articles twice.

1. That meeting was held at an abandoned theater in Fresno.
2. Green vineyards fill the valleys in California.
3. Plump grapes drooped on many vines.
4. César Chávez was good at solving a problem.
5. Imagination is required to find a nonviolent solution.
6. Chávez touched the new Italian suit.
7. Biographies are the stories of real people.
8. Hot sun baked the ground in Arizona.

**B** Write the adjectives in the sentences. Do not write the articles. Write whether each adjective tells *what kind, how many,* or *which one.*

  **1.** That family ate outside on warm nights.

  **2.** The little boy listened as aunts and uncles told magical tales.

  **3.** The Southwestern ranch had eighty acres of fertile land.

  **4.** The family had lived in this place for fifty years.

  **5.** For several years there was a terrible drought.

  **6.** The earth became dry and hard.

  **7.** Those people had to leave that life behind.

  **8.** The small Hispanic boy worked in the hot fields in California.

  **9.** By evening, every worker was exhausted.

 **10.** Most workers lived in substandard housing.

 **11.** The American dream was only a dream for these people.

 **12.** Thirty years later, the boy had become a great leader.

**C** Add your own adjectives and articles to complete each sentence. Write the sentences.

 **13.** ____ landowners treated their ____ workers badly.

 **14.** Children of these ____ workers missed ____ days of school.

 **15.** ___ man worked to improve ____ conditions for farmworkers.

 **16.** Their methods would be ____ strikes and ____ marches.

 **17.** ____ grapes in ____ vineyards were left to rot.

 **18.** ____ workers marched with ____ determination to spread the word.

 **19.** By the end of the march, ____ people had joined the cause.

 **20.** They earned ____ conditions for the workers.

# Test Preparation

✓ Write the letter of the adjective in each sentence.

1. A shy person will not speak in public.

   **A** shy     **C** speak
   **B** public    **D** will

2. That speech took courage and determination.

   **A** That     **C** and
   **B** courage   **D** took

3. The entire group listened carefully to his words.

   **A** group    **C** entire
   **B** words     **D** to

4. Some women wore shawls over their shoulders.

   **A** Some     **C** wore
   **B** women    **D** over

5. The Spanish language sounds musical to me.

   **A** me
   **B** language
   **C** musical
   **D** sounds

6. Do you think English is difficult?

   **A** English   **C** is
   **B** think     **D** difficult

7. Those boys need shoes and coats.

   **A** Those    **C** and
   **B** coats     **D** need

8. Fresh produce is brought by trucks to our stores.

   **A** brought   **C** Fresh
   **B** by       **D** stores

9. Hard-working laborers give us this abundance.

   **A** give
   **B** Hard-working
   **C** us
   **D** abundance

10. The majority of these workers are Mexican-American.

    **A** majority
    **B** Mexican-American
    **C** workers
    **D** are

# Review

✓ Write each sentence. Underline adjectives once and articles twice.

1. Most people do not like changes in the world.
2. Courageous, wise leaders must persuade us.
3. If we are comfortable, no change seems necessary.
4. The people who are miserable need help.
5. An action will affect the world in some way.
6. A person can help make the world a better place.
7. The task is not easy, but it is worthwhile.

✓ Write *a, an,* or *the* to complete each sentence. Choose the article that makes sense and follows the rules for articles.

8. _____ migrant workers organized a protest march.
9. Hundreds of people stood quietly and watched _____ marchers.
10. Dorothy watched them for more than _____ hour.
11. Then she worked for the rights of migrant workers for _____ lifetime.
12. Any person who tries to right wrongs is called _____ activist.

✓ Write the adjectives in the sentences. Do not write the articles. Write whether each adjective tells *what kind, how many,* or *which one.*

13. Six billion people live on the Earth.
14. Millions do not have clean water or decent food.
15. In some Asian countries, children work sixteen hours each day.
16. How can we solve those problems?
17. The leader's brave words inspired every listener.
18. These excited men and women will talk until dawn.
19. The future was looking bright.
20. Determined people can do wonderful things.

# Use Adjectives to Persuade

When trying to convince readers to agree with you, **use adjectives to persuade.** Adjectives can be used to make their subjects sound more positive or more negative. However, as with other opinions, you should support persuasive adjectives with facts.

**Descriptive Adjectives**
purple house, big truck, small shoes, thick smoke

**Persuasive Adjectives**
attractive house, monstrous truck, stylish shoes, obnoxious smoke

 Write the persuasive adjectives that the writer uses in the following paragraph.

**(1)** The grape farmers had unfair rules for their migrant workers. **(2)** Many noble grape pickers stood up against these written rules. **(3)** The farmers took unreasonable steps to stop the picketing. **(4)** There were violent confrontations between the wealthy farmers and the downtrodden workers. **(5)** Many people didn't get involved in the righteous conflict. **(6)** Were they too lazy, or were they biased?

 Write four sentences to support the following opinion. Use persuasive adjectives.

*Opinion:* Housework is unfair!

# Letter to the Editor

In a **letter to the editor,** a writer expresses his or her opinion on an issue. The letter is addressed to a newspaper or magazine and is intended for publication. The opinion should be elaborated with facts and examples.

**No Dumping!**

April 9, 2____

Dear Editor,

Writer states the issue and her feelings about it. → I am writing to you about the dangerous garbage dump being proposed by the city council. The city is planning to use vacant land between the river and the train tracks on the west side of the city as a new dump. This will not only be unpleasant for the surrounding neighborhoods, but also harmful to our environment and our wildlife.

Writer continues to use strong adjectives to express her opinions. → The proposed dump is to the west of our city. Since prevailing winds come out of the west, the putrid smell will blow across our city constantly. Furthermore, because the site is so close to the river, harmful pollutants can easily leach through the ground. This will make the water unlivable for fish, ducks, and

Opinions are supported with facts. → other wildlife.

Letter ends with call to action. → I urge the council to vote "no" on the dump location and to find a place better suited for it.

Sincerely,

Amy Rabideaux

# Demonstrative Adjectives

The adjectives *this, that, these* and *those* are called **demonstrative adjectives.** They describe which one or which ones. *This* and *that* modify singular nouns. *These* and *those* modify plural nouns. *This* and *these* refer to objects that are close by. *That* and *those* refer to objects farther away.

This myth is African. That myth we read last week is Chinese.

These clouds are small, but those clouds over there are huge.

- Do not use *here* or *there* after *this, that, these,* or *those.*

   **No**   This here animal eats grass. That there animal eats meat.

   **Yes**   This animal eats grass. That animal eats meat.

- Do not use *them* in place of *those.*

   **No**   Them stars twinkle in the sky.

   **Yes**   Those stars twinkle in the sky.

**A** Write the word in ( ) that completes each sentence correctly.

   **1.** (This, Those) great River ran across the continent of Africa.

   **2.** In the rich and plentiful land, (that, these) animals have everything they need.

   **3.** The grasses trail their roots in (that there, that) cool, clear river water.

   **4.** (Those, This) hyenas drink from the river every day.

   **5.** The people of Malawi created (this, them) myth.

   **6.** (These, That) wildebeest keeps running away from the sun.

   **7.** (These, This) sandy dunes were once grassy fields.

   **8.** The River wants to go to (those, these here) stars.

**B** Write *C* if the sentence is correct. If the sentence contains errors in the use of *this*, *that*, *these*, or *those*, write it correctly.

**1.** This here story is an example of a myth.

**2.** Them there shelves are filled with nonfiction books.

**3.** Did all of those early cultures create myths?

**4.** This fanciful tales occur in every civilization.

**5.** Those there myths were created by Greeks centuries ago.

**6.** In that distant past, people explained their world in myths.

**7.** These collection I am holding contains myths of Africa.

**8.** Do you remember that there Chinese myth we read last week?

**9.** The animals shown in this illustration can all talk and reason.

**10.** These art really brings the story to life.

**C** Replace the underlined word with the correct demonstrative adjective. Use the clue in ( ). Rewrite each sentence.

**11.** (far away) <u>The</u> mighty rivers in distant lands have a powerful hold on our imaginations.

**12.** (nearby) <u>The</u> book on South America has a whole chapter about the Amazon.

**13.** (nearby) <u>The</u> photographs of the Brazilian rainforest show brilliantly colored animals.

**14.** (far away) <u>The</u> spectacular waterfall makes the river seem like a living character.

**15.** (far away) Kasiya has retold <u>the</u> myths of the Malawi with skill and understanding.

# Test Preparation

☑ Write the letter of the demonstrative adjective that best completes each sentence.

1. _____ deer-like animal over there is an oryx.

   A  This      C  Them
   B  That      D  That there

2. _____ dark markings on the face help me identify it.

   A  Them      C  Those
   B  This      D  These here

3. _____ animal is also called a gemsbok.

   A  This        C  These
   B  That there  D  Those

4. _____ antelopes are larger than most other antelopes.

   A  This      C  This here
   B  That      D  These

5. In Africa, wildlife depends on _____ rivers that do not dry up.

   A  those     C  this
   B  that      D  these here

6. _____ elephants in the river are having a good time.

   A  Them      C  Those
   B  This      D  That

7. The giraffe spread _____ long legs wide and bent down to the water.

   A  them       C  this
   B  this here  D  those

8. _____ berries we picked look good, but are they poisonous?

   A  This here  C  That
   B  These      D  Them

9. _____ cockatoo in the tree over there has been eating them.

   A  These      C  That
   B  Them       D  Those here

10. _____ bamboo shoots taste delicious.

    A  These      C  This
    B  This here  D  That

# Review

✓ Write the word or words in ( ) that complete each sentence correctly.

1. Let's make an African mural to go with (this, these) myth.
2. I'll start at (this, this here) end of the wall, and you begin at (that, that there) one.
3. (Them, These) giraffes look awkward and graceful at the same time.
4. (These, Those) trees in the distance are acacia trees.
5. (That, Those) giraffe can reach the highest leaves.
6. Why do so many large mammals live on (these, this) savanna?
7. They find food in this grassland but not in (that, them) desert.
8. What kinds of animals live in (them there, those) mountains?
9. (This, Those) group of lions is called a pride.
10. (That, These) large lion with the heavy mane is the male.
11. (Those, that) adult elephants are protecting (that, those) baby elephant.
12. (That, This here) palm tree does not belong in (those, this) savanna scene.
13. I want to see more of (those, them) wildebeests.
14. Thousands of wildebeest cross (these here, these) plains at (those, this) time of year.

✓ Correct any mistakes in the use of demonstrative adjectives. Write the sentences correctly.

15. This here African safari is about to begin.
16. Please keep your hands and feet inside these vehicle at all times.
17. That there herd of animals in the distance is zebras.
18. Them animals are related to the horse, but they are not easily domesticated.

# Figurative Language

> **Figurative language** is the use of words apart from their
> ordinary meanings to add beauty and force. Three kinds of
> figurative language, or **figures of speech,** are simile, metaphor, and
> personification.
>
> • A *simile* is a figurative comparison that uses the word *like* or *as.*
> The wind was as gentle as a mother's voice.
>
> • A *metaphor* is a figurative comparison that does not use *like* or *as.*
> The cold wind was an icy sword.
>
> • *Personification* is figurative language that gives human qualities or
> actions to nonhuman things.
> The breeze sang a lullaby in the pines.

 Label each example of figurative language as *simile, metaphor,*
or *personification.*

   **1.** The stars were as bright as jewels.
   **2.** Alex's nose was a red cherry when he came inside.
   **3.** Ulla's smile wilted like day-old lettuce.
   **4.** The cactuses were pincushions.
   **5.** Tulips hung their heads in shame.
   **6.** The dry ground gratefully drank in the moisture.
   **7.** Tanya can be as pesky as poison ivy.
   **8.** The stream mumbled to itself as it ran over the rocks.

 Write a sentence about each object using figurative language. Use the
figure of speech indicated in ( ).

   **9.** black hair (simile)          **11.** wide river (metaphor)
   **10.** heavy backpack (simile)     **12.** strong wind (personification)

# Poem

A **poem** can express a writer's feelings and get readers to see things in new ways. Choose words carefully to create images, or mental pictures. You can also repeat sounds and arrange words on the page to emphasize ideas.

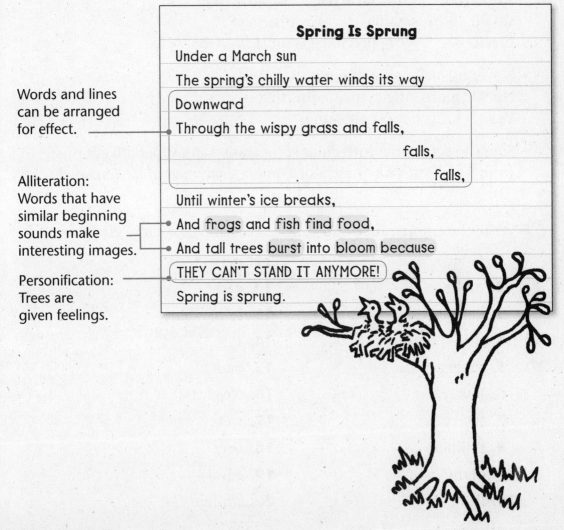

Words and lines can be arranged for effect.

Alliteration: Words that have similar beginning sounds make interesting images.

Personification: Trees are given feelings.

**Spring Is Sprung**

Under a March sun

The spring's chilly water winds its way

Downward

Through the wispy grass and falls,

          falls,

            falls,

Until winter's ice breaks,

And frogs and fish find food,

And tall trees burst into bloom because

THEY CAN'T STAND IT ANYMORE!

Spring is sprung.

# Comparative and Superlative Adjectives

**Comparative adjectives** are used to compare two people, places, things, or groups. Add *-er* to most short adjectives to make their comparative forms. Use *more* with longer adjectives. **Superlative adjectives** are used to compare three or more people, places, things, or groups. Add *-est* to most short adjectives to make their superlative forms. Use *most* with longer adjectives.

| Adjective | Comparative | Superlative |
|---|---|---|
| small | small<u>er</u> | small<u>est</u> |
| precious | <u>more</u> precious | <u>most</u> precious |

- Never use *more* or *most* with *-er* and *-est*.
  **No**    more longer, most amazingest
  **Yes**   longer, most amazing

- Some adjectives have irregular comparative and superlative forms: *good, better, best; bad, worse, worst; much, more, most; little, less, least.*

**A**  Write the comparative and superlative forms for each adjective.

| | | | |
|---|---|---|---|
| **1.** fancy | | **11.** perfect |
| **2.** much | | **12.** early |
| **3.** delicate | | **13.** remarkable |
| **4.** thin | | **14.** soft |
| **5.** rugged | | **15.** bad |
| **6.** lovely | | **16.** elegant |
| **7.** heavy | | **17.** wet |
| **8.** brilliant | | **18.** tiny |
| **9.** dense | | **19.** good |
| **10.** little | | **20.** strange |

**B** Write the correct adjective form or forms in ( ) to complete each sentence.

1. Is silver (more valuable, valuabler) than gold?
2. Of all the precious metals, I think gold is the (better, best).
3. Twenty-four carat gold is (more finer, finer) and (more softer, softer) than eighteen carat gold.
4. That prospector was (happiest, happier) than this one because he discovered gold.
5. Sam Dawson had the (worse, worst) luck of all the prospectors.
6. A few miners became wealthy, but (more, most) of the other prospectors were disappointed.
7. Merchants who sold goods to the miners became (more prosperous, prosperouser) than the miners.
8. Of all the miners, only the (luckier, luckiest) ones found rich veins of gold ore.
9. Lumps of gold called nuggets are the (purer, purest) natural form of the metal.
10. The rains were (heavier, heaviest) this year than last year; they made this the (wetter, wettest) spring on record.

**C** Write a sentence about the given topic. Use your own words and the adjective form indicated in ( ).

11. <u>big</u> vein of ore (superlative)
12. <u>beautiful</u> pendant (comparative)
13. <u>amazing</u> sight (superlative)
14. <u>smart</u> miner (comparative)
15. <u>shabby</u> cabin (superlative)

# Test Preparation

Write the letter of the adjective that correctly completes each sentence.

1. Many people think gold is the ____ investment of all.

   A better
   B more better
   C best
   D most best

2. ____ people may have more jewels than other people.

   A Most wealthiest
   B Wealthier
   C More wealthier
   D Most wealthier

3. The ____ china in the store was decorated with gold.

   A most fancier
   B more fancy
   C fanciest
   D most fanciest

4. Gold has ____ density than copper.

   A greatest
   B greater
   C more great
   D more greater

5. The gold-plated bracelet contains ____ gold than the solid gold one.

   A little
   B leastest
   C least
   D less

6. The brass plate was ____ than the copper one.

   A shinier
   B shiniest
   C more shinier
   D most shiniest

7. Never choose the ____ ring of all the rings in the tray.

   A cheaper
   B more cheaper
   C cheapest
   D most cheapest

8. That diamond is neither the best one nor the ____ one.

   A most bad
   B worst
   C worse
   D baddest

# Review

Write the comparative and superlative forms of each adjective.

1. lonely
2. fat
3. uncomfortable
4. silky
5. bad
6. compassionate
7. rainy
8. red
9. courageous
10. shy
11. pretty
12. proud
13. mysterious
14. good
15. reliable
16. much

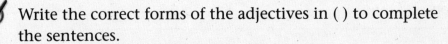

Write the correct forms of the adjectives in ( ) to complete the sentences.

17. The finish on the copper pans is (duller, more duller) than it was a year ago.

18. Adelaide polished the silver to make it (shinier, most shiniest).

19. The (plainer, more plain) silverware will be easier to shine.

20. The dining room was the (drafty, draftiest) room in the house.

21. Put the (more better, best) crystal vase on the table.

22. That fruit salad is the (deliciousest, most delicious) salad I have ever eaten.

23. I use (least, less) sugar than the amount that the recipe calls for.

24. The dinner guests became (more cheerful, cheerfuller) as the meal went on.

25. The engagement party was the (happier, happiest) event of the year.

# Visual Images

Good writing helps the reader "see" what is happening.
Writers create strong **visual images** by using exact and vivid
nouns, adjectives, verbs, and figures of speech.

**Weak**   Dr. Stedler cut the vines.

**Strong**   Dr. Stedler slashed through the thick curtain of vines.

Read the paragraph. Then find items in the box that give stronger
visual images than the underlined words. Write and number your
answers.

| | |
|---|---|
| struck dumb with amazement | inched their way |
| conquerors, scavengers, and thieves | gently laid |
| massive golden statue of an eagle | flickering glow |

   **(1)** Watching their step, Dr. Stedler and the other explorers <u>went</u>
into the cave. **(2)** The only light they had was the <u>light</u> of their
torches. **(3)** Then they saw it—a <u>large gold figure</u>. **(4)** Everyone was
<u>very quiet</u>. **(5)** How could <u>people</u> have left this treasure untouched?
**(6)** Dr. Stedler <u>put</u> a finger on the statue, and immediately a
tremendous groan filled the cave.

Write about a real or imaginary trip to a museum. Use strong visual
images to help the reader "see" what you "saw."

# Brochure

A museum **brochure** gives the reader information about artifacts in a museum. It also tries to persuade the reader to visit the museum to see the artifacts. A brochure is usually written in short paragraphs to make it easy to "digest."

First, give important facts.

Provide short paragraphs to describe pictures.

Give educational information in an interesting style.

Provide a persuasive "clincher."

**Discover Gold!**

Since the beginning of time, humans have been fascinated by the precious metal called gold. From now through August 23, the State History Museum invites you to view its rich new exhibit, *Gold: From Tutankhamen to the 2000s.*

*Mask of Tutankhamen* This mask was found in 1922 but created in the 14th century B.C. It adorned the coffin of the Egyptian pharaoh Tutankhamen.

*Roman Gold Coins* These coins date from before A.D. 79. Archaeologists found them in the ruins of Pompeii, still clutched in the hand of their owner.

*California Nugget* The California Gold Rush in 1849 brought thousands of people to the West. They were searching for valuable nuggets like this one.

*Gold Audio Adapters* Today gold's noncorrosive qualities are used in high-tech products, such as these audio adapters. How much gold is in *your* home?

*And more!* See these artifacts and more at the State History Museum, open seven days a week. Don't miss this golden opportunity!

# Adverbs

An **adverb** tells *how, when,* or *where* actions happen. An adverb may appear before or after the verb it modifies or between the parts of a verb phrase.

The boy walked <u>quietly</u> through the library.   (How)

He has <u>now</u> read the entire book.          (When)

<u>Outside</u> the traffic rumbled and roared.       (Where)

Adverbs such as *too, very, quite, really, so, nearly,* and *almost* can modify adjectives and other adverbs.

I was <u>almost</u> late. He reads <u>very</u> fast.

**Comparative adverbs** compare two actions. Add *-er* to most adverbs to make them comparative. **Superlative adverbs** compare three or more actions. Add *-est* to most adverbs to make them superlative. If an adverb ends in *-ly,* use *more* or *most* instead of *-er* or *-est.*

| | | |
|---|---|---|
| bright | brighter | brightest |
| carelessly | more carelessly | most carelessly |

Some adverbs have special comparative and superlative forms: *well, better, best; badly, worse, worst; much, more, most.*

**A** Write each sentence. Underline the adverb(s). Circle the word(s) each adverb modifies.

1. The caliph enthusiastically bought valuable books.

2. The new library is nearly completed.

3. The precious manuscripts are stored here.

4. Everywhere men sat and carefully read their books.

5. They shared their ideas very openly.

**B** If the sentence is correct, write *C*. If it contains an adverb error, rewrite the sentence and correct the error.

1. The translator worked rapid but accurately.
2. People in great civilizations have always valued wisdom.
3. Scholars thoughtful study the wise ideas and writings of past generations.
4. Baghdad once shone brightlyer than any other city in the ancient world.
5. The library safely harbored the greatest collection of knowledge in the world.
6. That particular manuscript is real old and priceless.
7. Ali learned most quickly than Ghassan.
8. Bev studied Arabic daily for three years.
9. She held the rare manuscript more respectful than a priceless crown of gold.
10. The university library was always quiet, but not too quiet.
11. The librarian turned the fragile pages of the old manuscript very slow.
12. Of all the library's possessions, this ancient book was handled more carefully.

**C** Rewrite each sentence. For each sentence, add an adverb that answers the question in ( ).

13. Some students study the night before a test. (How?)
14. Alison memorized key words and facts. (When?)
15. However, she will forget this information. (When?)
16. Real learning takes place when you understand something. (How?)
17. Plato taught Aristotle. (How?)
18. Aristotle went on to become a great teacher himself. (When?)
19. Aristotle's pupil Alexander revered his teacher. (How?)
20. We know this bright pupil as Alexander the Great. (When?)

# Test Preparation

✓ Write the letter of the correct adverb form to complete each sentence.

1. Of all the teachers, Ms. Lin spoke ____.

   **A** more clearly
   **B** most clearly
   **C** clearliest
   **D** clear

2. You know history ____ than I do.

   **A** well
   **B** good
   **C** best
   **D** better

3. Allen has traveled ____ in Europe than we have.

   **A** more often
   **B** often
   **C** oftener
   **D** more oftener

4. He ____ explores ancient castles.

   **A** frequent
   **B** frequently
   **C** frequenter
   **D** frequentest

5. The bus should have left at 8, but it left ____ than that.

   **A** latest
   **B** late
   **C** later
   **D** more late

6. Of all the grand castles, the oldest one sat ____ on its hill.

   **A** grander
   **B** more grandly
   **C** grand
   **D** most grandly

7. The tired travelers ____ climbed the stairs.

   **A** wearily
   **B** more weary
   **C** most wearier
   **D** weary

8. The children slept ____ of all the travelers.

   **A** very deep
   **B** very deeply
   **C** more deeply
   **D** most deeply

# Review

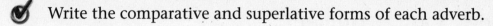 Write the comparative and superlative forms of each adverb.

1. happily
2. well
3. late
4. fast
5. cautiously

6. recently
7. remarkably
8. loud
9. much
10. proudly

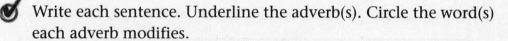 Write each sentence. Underline the adverb(s). Circle the word(s) each adverb modifies.

11. Peter always wanted a traveler's life.

12. He constantly read travel brochures and magazines.

13. Grass-roofed huts nestled cozily among palm trees.

14. Camels strolled lazily over the windswept desert.

15. The guide waited impatiently for him.

16. Peter worked toward his very important goal.

17. Adventure travel would certainly cost a great deal of money.

18. Finally, Peter had saved enough money.

19. He traveled often and learned quickly.

20. He wisely chose his favorite places and then planned his trips.

21. Peter now plans and leads adventure vacations for others.

22. His work makes him really happy.

23. Vivid Vacations has certainly enjoyed success.

24. Peter's customers praise his trips enthusiastically.

25. His business naturally brings him much contentment.

# Support Your Argument

> When you write to persuade, use convincing details to **support your argument.** Otherwise, the reader has no reason to agree with you! Follow up all assertions with supporting statements.

 Read the following advertisement. Write four supporting details from the ad that might persuade readers to stay at this resort.

---

*You Should Visit the Camembert Grand Hotel and Resort!*

Camembert Grand Hotel and Resort is a beautiful place to stay. It was built in 1929 and served as a playground for "the rich and famous" for twenty years. In 1998 it was repaired, beautified, and reopened. Last year this showplace was voted Canada's best vacation spot. The food is excellent! The resort is located 70 kilometers north of Ottawa, the capital of Canada. There are plenty of fun activities for the kids. Plan your next vacation at the Camembert Grand Hotel and Resort!

 Write three supporting statements for each assertion.

*Assertion:* Knowing how to read is important.

*Assertion:* Historical fiction is fun and educational.

*Assertion:* Every young person should stay in school and graduate from high school.

*Assertion:* Summer school should (should not) be eliminated.

# Ad

> An **advertisement** uses words and sometimes visual images to
> sell a product, service, or idea to the reader. An ad can appear in
> a magazine or newspaper, on a billboard, on television, or on the
> Internet. Ads are usually catchy, short, and to the point because ad
> space costs money!

Grab readers'
attention
with title. ———

Provide ———
descriptions
for visual
images.

Tell readers ———
why they
should buy
or use what
you're selling.

**Cover-to-Cover Adventure!**

(Playful drawing of a girl in the cockpit of a World
War I plane, reading a book about airplanes)

Take off! Libraries are your windows to the world.
Your local library has thousands of books for you
to read: fiction, nonfiction, even books on tape for
when you're on the go!

(Drawing of a boy sitting in a group of gorillas,
reading a book about gorillas. One gorilla is
scratching its head and looking confused.)

Get in the mix! If you can't find the book you're
looking for, ask the librarian! He or she can get it to
you the next day.

(Drawing of a family in a castle surrounded by fairy-
tale characters. The mom is reading to the children.)

There's fantastic fun for the whole family! Let your
imagination run wild at your local library.

Give readers
a call to
action. ———

Get into fun—visit your local library today!

# Modifiers

Adjectives, adverbs, and prepositional phrases are **modifiers,** words or groups of words that tell more about, or modify, other words. Adjectives modify nouns and pronouns. Adverbs modify verbs, adjectives, or other adverbs. Prepositional phrases can act as adjectives or adverbs.

> **As Adjective**  He read books <u>about knights</u>.
> **As Adverb**  He dreamed <u>about knights</u>.

- To avoid confusion, place modifiers close to the words they modify. Adjective phrases usually come right after the word they modify. Adverb phrases may appear right after a verb or at the beginning of a sentence.

- Meaning can be unclear if a modifier is misplaced.

> **No**  <u>Fair and sweet</u>, every knight needs a lady.
> **Yes**  Every knight needs a lady, <u>fair and sweet</u>.

- The position of *only* in a sentence can affect meaning. Place *only* directly before the word(s) it modifies.

*Example:*  <u>Only</u> she laughed at him. (Nobody else laughed at him.)

She <u>only</u> laughed at him. (She didn't do anything except laugh at him.)

She laughed <u>only</u> at him. (She laughed at no one else.)

**A** Write *adj., adv.,* or *prep. phrase* to identify each underlined modifier. Write *adj.* or *adv.* to identify how a prepositional phrase is used.

1. We watch a movie <u>about medieval knights</u>.
2. Two armies battle <u>fiercely</u>.
3. The scene is <u>noisy</u> and confusing.
4. The king swings his <u>heavy</u> sword.
5. One knight falls <u>to the ground</u>.

**B** Write each sentence. Underline adjectives once and adverbs twice. (Do not underline the articles *a, an,* and *the*.) Circle prepositional phrases.

1. A fierce dragon terrorized the good people of the kingdom.

2. The king quickly called his faithful knights around him.

3. "I will handsomely reward the one who slays the dragon."

4. The youngest knight stepped forward fearlessly.

5. He had a golden ring with magical powers.

6. On his fast horse, he rode from the castle.

7. Black smoke and flames rose from a mountain cave.

8. Sir Arnold cured the miserable dragon of his heartburn.

**C** Add the kind of modifier indicated in ( ) to each sentence. Reposition the misplaced modifiers that are in the final five sentences. Write the new sentences.

9. Fairy tales intrigued the children. (prepositional phrase)
10. The knight charged the dragon. (adjective)
11. Dragons bring good luck. (prepositional phrase)
12. King Arthur ruled England. (adverb)
13. Tales grew out of his legend. (adjective)
14. Camelot is a kingdom. (adjective and prepositional phrase)
15. Knights defended their king. (prepositional phrase and adverb)
16. She wore a gown to the feast with feathers.
17. We read about knights who lived long ago on the Internet.
18. The girl could only wed the man who saved her, no one else.
19. The knight saved the damsel with a sword.
20. Jon read late at night about medieval monsters in bed.

# Test Preparation

Write the letter of the choice that correctly identifies the underlined word or words in each sentence.

1. What makes a hero <u>admirable</u>?

    A  adj.
    B  adv.
    C  adj. prep. phrase
    D  adv. prep. phrase

2. Strength and goodness are often traits <u>of a hero</u>.

    A  adj.
    B  adv.
    C  adj. prep. phrase
    D  adv. prep. phrase

3. A hero doesn't <u>always</u> have to be handsome.

    A  adj.
    B  adv.
    C  adj. prep. phrase
    D  adv. prep. phrase

4. In animated films <u>of today</u>, heroes may be funny.

    A  adj.
    B  adv.
    C  adj. prep. phrase
    D  adv. prep. phrase

5. Shrek wins our hearts <u>with his ogre-like charm</u>.

    A  adj.
    B  adv.
    C  adj. prep. phrase
    D  adv. prep. phrase

6. For all his faults, Shrek is <u>good</u> and kind.

    A  adj.
    B  adv.
    C  adj. prep. phrase
    D  adv. prep. phrase

Write the letter of the sentence that has a misplaced modifier.

7. A  A loyal friend, others admire Shrek.
    B  They may argue and disagree at times.
    C  When they need him, they can count on Shrek.
    D  Shrek is a good and dependable friend.

8. A  Villains in today's movies are not always all bad.
    B  We may recognize their faults in ourselves.
    C  However, the villain steps over the line.
    D  Someone must defeat the villain of good character.

# Review

Write *adj.* or *adv.* to identify how the underlined prepositional phrase is used in each sentence.

1. A cluster of windmills stood <u>on the horizon</u>.
2. A breeze turned their arms <u>in lazy circles</u>.
3. The hooves <u>of the horses</u> made plopping sounds in the dust.
4. The knight <u>on his quest</u> looked for enemies everywhere.
5. <u>At sunset</u>, he believed he had found one.
6. He did not shrink <u>from his duty</u>.

Write each sentence. Underline adjectives once and adverbs twice. Circle prepositional phrases.

7. Windmills once were the main source of power.
8. They harnessed energy from the wind.
9. The rough millstones turned and ground grain into flour.
10. The meal had been freshly ground and smelled delicious.
11. Farmers from everywhere brought corn and wheat to the mill.
12. The heavy sacks of grain returned later as flour for baking.
13. Crisp, fragrant loaves of bread emerged magically from a great stone oven.
14. The smell of wood smoke made the knights hungry.

Rewrite each sentence fixing the misplaced modifier.

15. Enormous tables stood in the center of the stone floor of rough wood.
16. They just ate meat, no vegetables.

# Topic Sentence

> All the sentences in a paragraph should tell about one main idea. Often the main idea is stated in a **topic sentence.** This sentence may appear anywhere in the paragraph, but often it is the first sentence.

 Match the letter of each topic sentence with its details.

**Topic Sentences**

**A** La Mancha is an area of Spain you'll enjoy visiting.
**B** Knights were an important part of the feudal system.
**C** Sancho Panza was Don Quixote's faithful squire.
**D** Reading books feeds your imagination.

**Details**

**1.** Fought for the lords and monarch
Protected the serfs
Lived by the code of chivalry

**2.** Followed him everywhere
Vowed to stay with him
Helped him when he was hurt

**3.** Historical setting of *Don Quixote*
Castles and windmills still standing
Known for cheese making and vineyards

**4.** Learn about faraway places
Inspired Señor Quexada to become Don Quixote
Humor, drama, whimsy, and more

 Write two topic sentences about horses based on the following details: Can carry heavy loads; Gallop at very fast speeds; Are highly intelligent

# Symbolism

> A handshake, an American flag, and a red cross—these things have special meaning to most people because they are **symbols.** A symbol is an object, person, action, or situation that has a meaning of its own but suggests other meanings.

Topic sentence states symbolism of windmills.

Writer refers to specific things in the selection.

Writer gives a modern example of "windmills."

---

### Windmills Everywhere You Look

Don Quixote's windmills are symbols of the obstacles we meet in everyday life, whether imagined or real. A modern reader can view Quixote's battles and positive outlook as a lesson in survival.

Even though the hero's battles are comic, we identify with his efforts to face obstacles. When Quixote sees windmills, he views them as giants. Then he lowers his lance and attacks them head-on. I "battle windmills" every time I face a stack of homework or a difficult assignment. A positive attitude like Quixote's makes the battle easier.

Although he gets stuck on the sails and is tossed around by the windmills, Quixote inspires me. He rides off with dignity and hope. Like our hero, we need to believe in ourselves, even if we appear foolish at times. Whether it's windmill giants or mountains of homework, we should follow Quixote's attitude and tackle life as it comes.

---

# Conjunctions

A **conjunction** is a word that is used to join words, phrases, or sentences.

**Coordinating conjunctions** such as *and, but,* and *or* are used to combine two or more subjects, predicates, or sentences to make compound subjects, predicates, or sentences.

Chariot races <u>and</u> foot races were part of the games.

Athletes might perform in many sports <u>or</u> focus on one sport.

I wanted to see the long jump, <u>but</u> I was too late.

**Subordinating conjunctions** such as *because, if, when, although, before,* and *after* are used to link dependent clauses and independent clauses in complex sentences.

<u>Before</u> the games began, all wars stopped.

She is a good runner <u>because</u> she practices.

Ⓐ Write the coordinating conjunction in ( ) that correctly completes each sentence. Write *compound subject, compound predicate,* or *compound sentence* to identify the parts that the conjunction joins.

1. The Greeks made carvings on the walls (or, but) covered them with paintings instead.

2. *The Iliad* (but, and) *The Odyssey* are epic Greek poems.

3. Phoenician art (and, but) shipbuilding would be great subjects for our reports.

4. Free male citizens of Athens could vote on laws, (or, but) women and slaves could not.

5. The Minoan king Minos was supposedly the son of Zeus (and, or) therefore possessed special powers.

6. Was Athens the capital of ancient Greece, (and, or) was it Troy?

**B** Write the conjunction in each sentence. Write *CC* if it is a coordinating conjunction and *SC* if it is a subordinating conjunction

1. There will be a ceremony before the games begin.
2. Will the athletes march in through the east or the west gate?
3. He carried his country's flag with pride and honor.
4. If she makes this jump, she will win a gold medal.
5. Athletes train for years but can lose by a fraction of a second.
6. Perhaps they will relax after they complete their events.
7. The Swiss team will win the silver or the bronze medal.
8. The Olympic Games inspire greatness because they test the abilities of the world's best athletes.

**C** Rewrite the following paragraph. Combine related subjects, predicates, or sentences using conjunctions to make the paragraph smoother. Where appropriate, drop repeated words or replace repeated nouns with pronouns.

**(9)** The Minoan civilization arose on the island of Crete around 2200 B.C. The Minoan civilization came to an end around 1450 B.C. **(10)** We know about this civilization. Archaeologists have uncovered Minoan palaces. **(11)** Beautiful paintings on the palace walls show happy, peaceful people. The paintings also show a country with strong sea power. **(12)** The Minoans wrote in a type of hieroglyphics. No one has been able to translate it yet.

# Test Preparation

☑ Write the letter of the conjunction(s) that best complete each sentence.

1. Spartan soldiers were disciplined ____ aggressive.

   A and        C when
   B after       D because

2. Spartan boys lived in military training camps, ____ girls lived at home.

   A before      C until
   B but         D if

3. ____ they were given little food, they had to fend for themselves.

   A Until       C Because
   B Or          D Although

4. Both boys ____ girls trained hard and were superb athletes.

   A so          C but
   B after        D and

5. ____ he trained for years, every boy would become a soldier.

   A After       C Unless
   B Or          D But

6. Sparta ____ Athens were quite different ____ both were Greek city-states.

   A or, if
   B and, because
   C but, until
   D and, although

7. Athenians were open to new ideas, ____ Spartans avoided change.

   A until       C because
   B but         D or

8. ____ the wealthy ruled Sparta, an elected assembly made decisions in Athens.

   A And         C While
   B If          D But

9. Spartan soldiers were famous for their skill ____ bravery in battle.

   A and         C but
   B if          D when

10. Athens ____ Sparta battled for 27 years ____ Athens finally surrendered.

    A and, until
    B but, because
    C or, after
    D and, so

# Review

 Write the coordinating conjunction in ( ) that correctly completes each sentence.

1. I like history, (and, but) I prefer literature.
2. Did you read *The Iliad,* (but, or) did you choose the myths?
3. *The Iliad* (and, or) *The Odyssey* are the most famous Greek epics.
4. Is Odysseus (but, or) Paris the hero of *The Odyssey*?
5. Odysseus (and, or) his men sailed the Mediterranean for years.
6. They had many exciting adventures, (or, but) their real goal was to return home.
7. Once they were trapped by a one-eyed monster named Cyclops, (and, or) many men were lost.
8. Odysseus was not perfect, (and, but) he was certainly clever and larger than life.

 Write the conjunction in each sentence. Write *CC* if it is a coordinating conjunction. Write *SC* if it is a subordinating conjunction.

9. The Romans conquered the Greeks, but they adopted much of the Greek culture.
10. Because the Romans admired Greek art, they used it in many of their creations.
11. The gods and goddesses of Greek mythology appear in Roman mythology too.
12. Was Poseidon or Neptune the Roman god of the sea?
13. While Zeus was the chief god of the Greeks, the Romans called him Jupiter.
14. Before Venus ruled as Roman goddess of love, she was called Aphrodite by the Greeks.

# Paraphrase

When you take notes on facts in a book or article, you **paraphrase** information. To paraphrase, choose the most important facts and restate them in your own words.

- Paraphrase only the main ideas, not unimportant details. Make sure you paraphrase the facts correctly.
- Use your own words, not the words and word order used by the author.
- If a phrase or sentence is especially interesting, write it in quotation marks.

Read the paragraph below. Write the letter of the sentence that is the best paraphrase of the paragraph.

Women in Athens were not citizens and could not participate in the assembly, vote, or serve on juries. In wealthy families, women were educated to run the household. In poor families, they worked alongside men as laborers.

**A** Wealthy Athenian women had more rights than poor Athenian women.

**B** Athenian women were much like slaves, for they could not vote or hold office.

**C** In Athens, women had neither citizenship nor a voice in government but managed the home or labored.

**D** You would not like to be a woman in ancient Greece.

Write a paraphrase for the paragraph below.

Pericles was the leader of Athens from 461 to 429 B.C. He supported democracy. He also started a system of payment for government service. The earlier system did not pay government workers.

# Taking Notes

**Taking good notes** is important for any research report. Without notes, you could not remember what you read and where you read it. Good notes include the important ideas written in an organized way and information about the source, including the title, the author's name, and the page numbers. The notes below are based on a chapter in a history book.

Source information is included for later use.

Notes are short and written in the order of reading.

Direct quotations have quotation marks.

**Notes on *Ancient Greece*, Chapter 1**

Ancient Greece by Kim Covert

Chapter 1, Ancient Olympics, pages 678–679

1. Events

   Running and chariot races

   Wrestling, boxing, pentathlon (incl. discus, javelin, long jump)

   Wreath of olive leaves to winner

2. History

   First recorded Olympics: 776 B.C. in Olympia, Greece

   Honored Zeus, ruler of Olympian gods

   Every 4 years for 1,000 years

   All wars stopped during Olympics

3. Ancient Greece "called the cradle of Western civilization"

   Government, art, architecture, literature, science, drama, athletics

   "The modern Olympics are one of many traditions developed in Greece."

# Commas

You already know some uses of **commas,** such as with words in a series and in compound sentences. Here are some more uses.

- After an introductory word or phrase, such as *well* or *yes*:
  By the way, I want to stop at the store. Yes, let's go.

- To set off a noun of direct address:
  Mrs. Lin, come in. I hope, sir, you will join us.

- After a dependent clause at the beginning of a sentence:
  Because he was shy, Tom was uneasy in crowds.

- Before and/or after an appositive—a noun or noun phrase describing another noun:
  The waiter, a refined gentleman, wore a tuxedo.

- Before and after interrupting words or phrases:
  Prawns, as you may know, are shrimp.

- Between a day of the week and a month and between a date and a year:
  The party is Saturday, June 1. Their wedding was on December 12, 2007.

- Between the street address and the city and between the city and the state in an address, but *not* before the ZIP code:
  She lives at 99 North Street, Little Rock, AR 72204.

**A** Write the parts of the letter. Add commas where they are needed.

**1.** Saturday September 6

**2.** Dear Meg

**3.** O'Fallon Illinois 62269

**4.** Meg how are you?

**5.** This summer by the way we will go to China Japan and India.

**6.** Yes I have to pinch myself but it is happening.

**B** Write each sentence. Add commas where they are needed.

1. Han what can you tell us about Chinese food?
2. I can make egg rolls wonton soup and sweet and sour chicken.
3. Hop's Chinese Restaurant is located at 1034 Peach Road DeKalb GA.
4. The bowling banquet always a favorite of mine will be held there on Friday October 13.
5. Will you pass the sauce Barb when you get a chance?
6. General Tsao's chicken the most popular item on the menu is both spicy and sweet.
7. Mr. Ta will you teach Marie Paul and me how to make fortune cookies for our party?
8. The letter was dated February 12 1944 and it began "Dear Hal You must come and visit."

**C** Write sentences with the parts described in ( ). Be sure to use commas correctly to set off these parts.

9. (appositive)
10. (interrupting word or phrase)
11. (dependent clause at beginning of sentence)
12. (noun of direct address)
13. (introductory word or phrase)
14. (complete mailing address)
15. (day, month, date, and year)

# Test Preparation

☑ Write the letter of the item that completes each sentence correctly.

**1.** The dinner party is on ____.

   **A** Saturday September 30

   **B** Saturday September, 30

   **C** Saturday, September, 30

   **D** Saturday, September 30

**2.** We will serve ____.

   **A** salad, lasagna, and rolls

   **B** salad, lasagna and rolls

   **C** salad, lasagna and, rolls

   **D** salad lasagna, and rolls

**3.** RSVP to 510 ____.

   **A** Mesa Austin TX, 78730

   **B** Mesa, Austin, TX 78730

   **C** Mesa Austin, TX, 78730

   **D** Mesa, Austin, TX, 78730

**4.** Karen ____ taught me etiquette.

   **A** Xidis my favorite aunt

   **B** Xidis, my favorite aunt

   **C** Xidis, my favorite aunt,

   **D** Xidis, my favorite, aunt

**5.** Which one is ____?

   **A** the salad fork, Bree

   **B** the, salad fork Bree

   **C** the salad fork Bree

   **D** the salad, fork Bree

**6.** After the ____ will be served.

   **A** soup, is cleared salad

   **B** soup is cleared salad,

   **C** soup is cleared salad

   **D** soup is cleared, salad

**7.** Please ____ at our table.

   **A** join us Casey

   **B** join us, Casey,

   **C** join us, Casey

   **D** join us Casey,

**8.** The ____ are seafood.

   **A** scallops, as I said,

   **B** scallops as I said,

   **C** scallops, as I said

   **D** scallops as I said

# Review

 Write the parts of the letter. Add commas where they are needed.

1. Dear Todd
2. 613 Taylor Drive Blythewood SC 29016
3. My flight arrives Monday November 20 2008.
4. I can't wait to see you Todd!
5. I will stay a whole week and I hope we can go hiking.

 Write each sentence. Add commas where they are needed.

6. We learned origami the Japanese art of paper folding.
7. Ashley is that a crane you have made?
8. Zach arranged seashells and Brent carved driftwood.
9. The bouquet contained roses daisies and larkspur.
10. If you will help me I will try eating with chopsticks.
11. Yes I did drop that piece of chicken on the floor.
12. No Sam I don't think you should spear the fish with your chopsticks.

Rewrite each sentence. Add commas where they are needed. Delete any unnecessary commas.

13. Frank traveled, to India Indochina and Australia.
14. The trip began on Wednesday July 12 and, it ended on Sunday August 20.
15. Would you, rather travel on your vacation Tonia or stay in one interesting place?

# Strong Conclusions

> A **strong conclusion** summarizes your ideas in a memorable way that keeps your message in your reader's mind. A good conclusion should be more than just a restatement of what went before. It could provide an insight, present a twist, or pose a challenge or a question to readers.

 Read the following paragraph and the four possible conclusions. Write the letter of the sentence that is the strongest conclusion for the paragraph. Then explain your choice.

Always try to be a good guest when you visit another country. Some customs and foods may seem strange. Keep an open mind and try them. Some of your habits might strike your hosts as rude or odd. If possible, learn about the proper way to behave in your host country.

**Possible Conclusions**

**A** In summary, be polite and observant when you are a visitor.

**B** People who are rude tourists give Americans a bad reputation.

**C** Making mistakes in another country can be embarrassing.

**D** If you know about a country and its people, both you and they are likely to enjoy your visit.

 Write a strong conclusion for the following paragraph.

Immigrants to America have brought us a wealth of new foods. Strudel is a delicious pastry introduced by German newcomers. Shish kebab comes to us courtesy of the Turks. If you enjoy a fragrant curry, thank the immigrants from India.

# Newsletter

A **newsletter article** should be fairly brief, focused, and directed to an audience likely to read the newsletter. The style is usually informal and friendly. The following article was written for a monthly newsletter called *Zoo News*.

**Lori Manz, Employee of the Month**

First two sentences grab readers' attention.

Lori Manz is being watched as she walks toward her charges. They get a good view since they have eyes on both sides of their heads. Lori is a zookeeper at the reptile house at Hill Street Zoo.

Quotations show that Lori knows and cares about snakes.

"I have always found snakes beautiful and fascinating," Lori says. "Throughout history, snakes have been the subjects of many myths and superstitions. Some cultures even honor them."

Lori is responsible for feeding, cleaning, and watching over the snakes and other reptiles. Every morning she checks each snake. If one looks unhealthy, she contacts the zoo veterinarian. How does she examine

Article mentions special tools needed on the job.

a poisonous snake? She uses a snake hook to get it out of the cage and wears leather gloves to hold it down.

Writer ends with a strong conclusion.

*Zoo News* salutes Lori for her latest effort— bringing snakes and other reptiles to the Children's Zoo. Her class, titled "Slithers and Scales," introduces kids to her beloved reptiles.

# Quotations and Quotation Marks

A **direct quotation** gives a speaker's exact words. Begin each quotation with a capital letter and enclose it in **quotation marks.** Use commas to set off words that introduce, interrupt, or follow a direct quotation. Place the end punctuation or the comma that ends the quotation inside the quotation marks.

"Are you going to the festival tonight?" I asked. "I will go," he replied.

Do not begin the second part of an interrupted quotation with a capital letter. Set off the interrupting words with commas.

"My baby is ill," said the woman, "so I can't attend."

If the interrupted quotation is two complete sentences, use a period and a capital letter.

"Look at that warrior," I said. "He is brave."

An **indirect quotation** is a quotation that is reworded instead of being quoted directly. It does not need quotation marks.

Sara said she was going to the festival.

**A** Write *I* if the sentence is punctuated or capitalized incorrectly. Write *C* if the sentence is correct.

1. "When you study Aztec history" said Mr. Dale, "you will learn about Montezuma."
2. "We burned the temple as a sign to the world," boasted the warrior.
3. The warrior shouted, "Round up the captives"!
4. "I am an Eagle warrior," he said, "And my brother is a Jaguar."
5. "Put this gold in the treasury," he ordered. "Montezuma will be pleased."

**B** If a sentence needs quotation marks and other punctuation, rewrite it correctly. If it does not need corrections, write *C*.

1. What do you know about the Aztec kingdom asked Mr. Hadley.
2. They had a wealthy civilization said Aaron and they built a city on a lake.
3. Jahlil said he thought their temples were interesting.
4. Mr. Hadley remarked Tenochtitlán was an Aztec city built by making an island on a shallow lake.
5. It had canals, streets, causeways, and a great temple at the center he added.
6. The system of canals was brilliant said Alice because it provided constant irrigation for crops.

**C** Write the following paragraph. Add quotation marks, punctuation, and capitalization. Use a paragraph indent to indicate each time the speaker changes.

How did the Aztec empire end asked Will. It fell to Spanish conquistadors Mom replied. They were adventurer-soldiers with armies in search of wealth. The Aztecs were warriors said Will why couldn't they beat the Spanish? They lacked the guns, cannons, and horses of the Spaniards Mom explained and Montezuma believed the leader Cortés might be a god. That's ridiculous Will hooted how could he believe that a person was a god? It was 1519 she went on and in that year the Aztecs believed the exiled god Quetzalcoatl would return to reclaim his throne.

# Test Preparation

 Write the letter of the item that correctly completes each sentence.

1. "Are those Aztec or Mayan
   ____ asked Mary.

   A  ruins,"
   B  ruins?"
   C  ruins?,"
   D  ruins"

2. Ellen ____ cultures built step
   pyramids."

   A  said, Both
   B  said, "both
   C  said. "Both
   D  said, "Both

3. "I think," added ____ were
   built after the Egyptian
   pyramids."

   A  Jorge, "these
   B  Jorge. "These
   C  Jorge "these
   D  Jorge, these

4. "Often a temple was built on
   ____ said Ms. Gramley.

   A  top,"
   B  top"?
   C  top"
   D  top."

5. "It was used for religious
   purposes," she ____ served as
   a landmark."

   A  continued "and
   B  continued "And
   C  continued, "and
   D  continued. "And

6. ____ noted Buddy. "It has
   steps on all four sides."

   A  "Cool"
   B  "Cool!"
   C  "cool,"
   D  "cool"

7. "Each set has 91 steps," she
   went ____ one for almost
   each day of the year."

   A  on. "That's
   B  on, "that's
   C  on. That's
   D  on, that's

8. "Step pyramids were meant
   to be ____ told us.

   A  climbed." she
   B  climbed," she
   C  climbed" she
   D  climbed," She

# Review

 Rewrite each sentence. Add quotation marks and punctuation as needed.

1. Would you like to end our Aztec study with a feast asked Ms. Nissing

2. Hurray we shouted. What shall we eat

3. We should have fresh, hot tortilla pancakes suggested Rosa

4. Didn't the Aztecs drink chocolate Drew asked

5. Yes replied Ms. Nissing but it wasn't like our hot cocoa

6. She said that corn, beans, and squash were common foods of the Aztecs

7. Let's dress up like the Aztecs too offered Danielle

8. Ms. Nissing suggested that we wear jewelry made of gold, silver, jade, or seashells

 Rewrite each sentence, adding quotation marks, capitalization, and punctuation as needed.

9. European soldiers of the 1500s wore armor and carried metal weapons Mr. Pappas said

10. The metal protected them well he added but it was incredibly hot and heavy

11. Can you imagine the battle asked Sean between the Aztec warriors and the Spanish conquistadors

12. The native warriors were armed with clubs, bows and arrows, and spears said Una they didn't have armor, though

13. In the city of Tenochtitlán added Brad the Aztec warriors could also fight from swift-moving canoes

14. Mr. Pappas told us that the Aztecs were doomed to lose the war to the Spaniards

**WRITER'S CRAFT**

# Include Important Details

When you write a research report, use the facts in your outline. Keep your topic, audience, and purpose in mind. Then **include the important details** about your topic.

Below is part of an outline and a paragraph based on it. Write the sentences in this paragraph that have unimportant details.

**B.** Agriculture
1. Slash-and-burn: crops planted in clearing of burned part of forest
2. *Chinampas:* mud built up out of swamps to form fertile islands
3. Corn most important; avocados, beans, squash, papayas, cacao beans

The Aztec were excellent farmers. They used slash-and-burn methods, burning part of the forest and planting crops in the fertile ashes. They created *chinampas* by digging mud out of swamps and planting crops on these islands. *Chinampas* would be good for swampy areas today. The Aztecs' most important crop was corn. In addition, they grew avocados, beans, squash, papayas, and cacao beans. These foods are still popular.

 Write about the Aztec city of Tenochtitlán using the following details from an outline.

1. On five islands in Lake Texcoco
2. No roads; canals for canoes
3. Population: 200,000 people
4. Spanish explorers: "Venice of the New World"

# Outlining

An **outline** is a way to summarize and organize information in a text. Main ideas are listed with Roman numerals (I, II, III, IV). Details that support each main idea are listed with the letters A, B, C, and so on. An outline helps you put your ideas in order before you write a research report. Here is one student's outline on an article about the Aztec city, Tenochtitlán.

Outline is divided into three parts: Introduction, Body, Conclusion

There are always at least two items in a section.

Subtopics support main topics.

### The Aztec News, Tenochtitlán, A Guide

**I.  Introduction:** Tenochtitlán is a large, beautiful city that attracts many visitors.
  **A.** It is surrounded by mountains and water.
  **B.** It is home to more than 250,000 people.
  **C.** You can travel by dugout canoes or walk along a causeway.

**II.  Body:** You'll enjoy the sights, food and markets, and festivals.
  **A.** Sights
    **1.** Visit the Great Temple and its shrines.
    **2.** See cottages outside city center.
  **B.** Food and Markets
    **1.** Buy pancakes from street vendors and drink water from fresh mountain springs.
    **2.** Visit Tlatelolco Market.
  **C.** Religious Festivals
    **1.** They are held monthly.
    **2.** Costumes, dancing, and music are spectacular.

**III.** **Conclusion:** Make your visit to Tenochtitlán a trip to remember!

# Punctuation

- A **semicolon (;)** can be used instead of a comma and a conjunction to join two independent clauses.

  Mr. Li moved to Chicago; he looked for a house.

- Semicolons separate items in a series if commas are already used in the series.

  The band includes John Drummond, horn; Tim Salmonson, piano; and Jim Smelser, drums.

- A **colon (:)** is used after the salutation in a business letter and to separate hours and minutes in expressions of time.

  Dear Sir:      12:01 P.M.

- Colons introduce a list and set off a speaker's name in a play.

  The train stops in the following cities: Jackson, Little Rock, and Chicago.

  JOHN: I can't wait to start my new job.

- A **dash (—)** sets off information that interrupts the flow of a sentence.

  Jon Bixly—he's written a book—is an authority on the early 1900s.

- A **hyphen (-)** joins compound adjectives before nouns, spelled-out numbers, and some two-word nouns.

  a well-cooked goose      forty-three      self-control

**A** Rewrite each sentence. Add the missing punctuation marks.

1. I have visited these states Idaho, Montana, and Colorado.
2. Mr. Thomas he was running late caught the 504 P.M. train.
3. We found seats on the train thirty two people had to stand.
4. This train will stop in Nashville, Tennessee Louisville, Kentucky and Indianapolis, Indiana.

**B** Match each item in the box with a numbered item to form a logical sentence. Write the sentences, adding colons or semicolons as needed.

---

one of her paintings sold for more than a million dollars

a number 2 pencil, a calculator, and a bottle of water

We hope you will approve our health fair plan

I plan to specialize in oncology

Aurora, Illinois Waco, Texas and Wilmington, North Carolina

---

1. For the test you will need the following
2. I have lived in these towns
3. Dear Principal Breen
4. The artist had become famous
5. I hope to be a doctor someday

**C** Add hyphens, dashes, colons, and semicolons to the following sentences. Rewrite the sentences.

6. The number 12 train on the Blue Line that's the one I take to work arrives in Chicago at 837 A.M.

7. You'll find the train a first rate choice for commuting it never gets stuck in rush hour traffic.

8. Fifty two riders signed the petition that began "Dear Mayor Katz We protest the closing of Lincoln School."

9. The empire fell for these reasons corrupt leaders, social disorganization, and an epidemic of plague.

10. I especially enjoy an action packed, fast paced adventure tale.

# Test Preparation

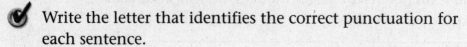 Write the letter that identifies the correct punctuation for each sentence.

1. The long awaited day of departure finally had arrived.

   A   long-awaited
   B   day—of departure
   C   awaited;
   D   departure:

2. Five people waited on the platform they carried all their possessions.

   A   on the platform—
   B   on the platform;
   C   waited:
   D   waited-on

3. They had been sharecroppers you know the term all their lives.

   A   sharecroppers;
   B   sharecroppers-you
   C   —you know the term—
   D   term:

4. Jeremiah would search for work for thirty two days.

   A   —for thirty two days—
   B   days;
   C   for work:
   D   thirty-two

5. Dear Sir I would like to apply for a job as a night watchman.

   A   Dear Sir:
   B   for a job;
   C   —as a night watchman—
   D   I would like:

6. EMPLOYER Tell me about your work experience.

   A   —about your work—
   B   Tell me,
   C   EMPLOYER:
   D   EMPLOYER;

7. The list included these jobs cook, carpenter, and gardener.

   A   jobs—cook
   B   jobs:
   C   jobs;
   D   these-jobs

8. He will start work at 730 A.M.

   A   will—
   B   work:
   C   start-work
   D   7:30

# Review

 Rewrite each sentence. Add the missing punctuation marks.

1. A new life awaited the travelers none of them knew what that life would be like.

2. One family had spread out these foods chicken, biscuits, pickles, and corn on the cob.

3. The baby she was cutting teeth fussed and fretted the whole way.

4. Dear Passengers For safety reasons, all windows are to be kept closed and locked.

5. Your ticket entitles you to these items a seat in the main cabin, a beverage, and a snack.

6. The well paid employees of Smith Construction held on to their jobs.

7. PANSY But where will we live? How will we survive?
   JOB We'll stay with my cousin 'til we find a place.

8. The children were exhausted they soon fell fast asleep on the bench seats.

9. Their parents were hopeful but anxious they sat up the whole night and watched the towns passing.

10. At 629 A.M. the train pulled into Union Station.

11. They gazed up in awe they had never seen a skyscraper as they walked the city streets.

12. Pick one of these dates for the church picnic Sunday, July 10 Saturday, July 16 or Sunday, July 17.

13. A well known activist would speak first.

14. The pace of life in the city was rapid they would have to adjust.

15. The worn out visitors walked twenty seven blocks to their hotel.

# Stick to the Subject

When writing a job application, you should have one focus— getting the job. Employers have only a limited time to read many applications, so it's important that your answers **stick to the subject.** A brief, focused answer demonstrates that you understand the question and can communicate effectively in writing.

 Write any information in the answers below that strays from the subject of the question.

1. *Explain why you want this job at Technocraft.*

   That's a good question! I want this job because it gives me an opportunity to put my math skills to good use. Furthermore, I am knowledgeable about technology and would like to share this information with customers.

2. *What skills do you have that are related to this telemarketing job?*

   I communicate well verbally, and I am fluent in Spanish. I can ride a bicycle. My voice is clear, and I can be persuasive.

3. *What are your strengths?*

   My strengths are my creativity and calmness. It's easy for me to figure out ways to solve problems. Also, it's hard to make me panic. If there is an emergency at work, I'm sure I can keep a cool head. I used to oversleep, but that won't happen now with my new digital alarm clock.

 Answer the following question. Remember to stick to the subject.

   *If you saw another employee stealing from the store, what would you do?*

# Job Application

Besides information such as your name, address, phone number, and previous work experience, a **job application** may ask you to write a short essay about yourself. This is your chance to say why *you* should be hired for the job.

**Tell Us About Yourself**

Explain why you would be a good person for the job.

I think I would be an ideal candidate for the job of camp counselor at Wolverine Summer Camp. My abilities, experience, and interests fit perfectly with your job description.

Show how your interests and experience fit the job.

I am just about to finish sixth grade at Carver Middle School, where my favorite classes are language arts, art, and P.E. These classes, for which I receive good grades, show that I communicate well with others, have a knack for arts and crafts, and love being active in the outdoors.

In addition, I have experience as a babysitter and enjoy working with children. As I stated earlier in the application, I have tutored third graders in reading for a year.

A strong conclusion makes you stand out.

I have been a camper at Wolverine Summer Camp for the last five summers, so I know what it takes to be a good camp counselor. I look forward to the opportunity to use my experience, interests, and talents to make camp a fun learning experience for a new generation of Wolverines!

# Taking Tests

## TIPS FOR WRITING FOR TESTS

Follow these tips when writing for a test:

# Before Writing

- Read the prompt carefully. What does it ask you to do?
- Write down key words that name your audience *(warn <u>people who eat junk food</u>)*, state the purpose of the composition *(<u>give directions</u>)*, and tell you how to organize your points *(provide <u>step-by-step instructions</u>)*.
- Use a graphic organizer to plan your composition.
- Determine the tone of your writing (friendly, formal).

# During Writing

- Reread the prompt as you write to make sure you are on topic.
- Keep in mind your graphic organizer and stay focused.
- Write a good beginning. You might engage readers with a thought-provoking question or an interesting fact.
- Develop and elaborate ideas. Support your main idea, your observations, or your opinion.
- Write a strong ending. Try to write a "clincher" sentence to provide a clear ending. You might add a final comment of your own or challenge your reader with a command.

# After Writing

- Check your grammar and mechanics (punctuation, spelling).
- Reread the prompt and review your work. There's still time to add words or correct errors.

# Writing a Personal Narrative

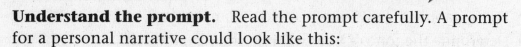

> A **test** may ask you to write a personal narrative. Your narrative should have a beginning, middle, and end. Use words that capture your voice, feelings, and point of view. Follow the tips below.

**Understand the prompt.**  Read the prompt carefully. A prompt for a personal narrative could look like this:

> Write a personal narrative about an interesting adventure or difficult experience in your life. Use the words *I* and *me*.

Key words and phrases are *personal narrative, adventure,* and *difficult experience.*

**Find a good topic.**  Choose an event that you recall in some detail. Consider a visit, a lost pet, or a fun discovery.

**Organize your ideas.**  Make a story organizer on scratch paper.

| Event | first ride on motorcycle |
|---|---|
| **Where and when** | country road, last July |
| **Details** | surprised me<br>purr of motor, rush of wind<br>feeling close to nature and traffic |
| **How it ended** | tired but happy |

**Write a good beginning.**  Set the tone with your first sentence.

**Develop and elaborate ideas.**  Use the information in your organizer. Include vivid details and varied sentences.

**Write a strong ending.** Make the ending powerful and vivid.

**Check your work.** Make any necessary changes. See how the personal narrative below addresses the prompt.

If there is one thing I can count on, it's that Aunt Sass will surprise me. Last July she called and said, "I'll be over to take you for a ride." She pulled into our parking lot on a shiny new red motorcycle!

I breathed in the smell of leather and engine oil. I could hardly wait to hop on. First, Aunt Sass showed me how to sit and hold on safely and put on my helmet. Then we were off! At first, I was nervous because the traffic was right there in my face. We seemed to be flying.

Soon we puttered down a country road, and I began to relax my grip on Aunt Sass's waist. The grass, trees, and fresh air smelled wonderful. I could see blue wildflowers along the road and goats grazing in a field. The world seemed closer and more focused.

When I got off the motorcycle, I was tired but happy. I'd had another amazing adventure with Aunt Sass.

1. The opening sentence creates interest and anticipation.
2. The writer uses personal pronouns to express feelings.
3. Details appeal to readers' senses.
4. Connectors establish the order of events.
5. The ending ties back to the beginning.

# Writing a How-to Report

> A **test** may ask you to explain how to do or make something. Include all the steps. Use words such as *next* and *last* to show the order of the steps. Follow the tips below.

**Understand the prompt.**   Read the prompt carefully. A prompt for a how-to report may look like this:

Write a report that gives steps on how to make or do something. Make your report easy to understand. Explain all the steps and materials that are needed.

Key words and phrases are *report, steps, how to make or do something,* and *all the steps and materials.*

**Find a good topic.**   Choose something you can make or do well and explain easily, such as a simple meal or a game.

**Organize your ideas.**   Make a how-to chart with the name of your task, the materials, and the steps.

| Task | Make pot pie—a colonial meal |
|---|---|
| Materials | chicken, chicken bouillon, onions, potatoes, carrots, corn, peas, frozen pie crusts, knife, cutting board, pan |
| Steps | 1. Cut up chicken. 2. Chop onions, carrots, potatoes. 3. Cook vegetables and chicken in bouillon. 4. Thaw crusts. 5. Pour mixture into one crust; cover with second crust. 6. Bake an hour at 375°F. |

**Write a good beginning.**   State the task clearly.

**Develop and elaborate ideas.**   Use the steps in your chart.

**Write a strong ending.** You might add a personal comment.

**Check your work.** Is any information missing? See how the how-to report below addresses the prompt.

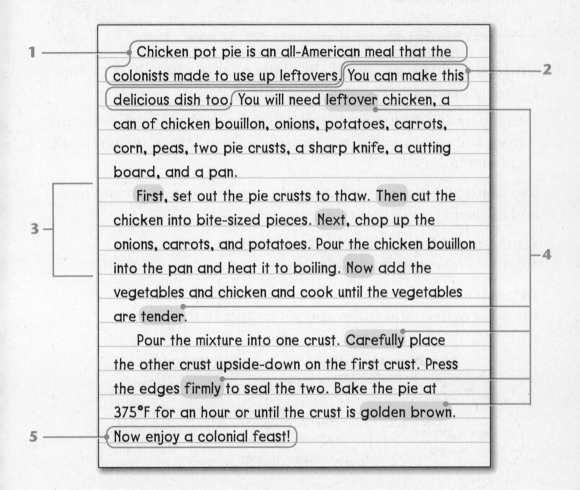

1. Chicken pot pie is an all-American meal that the colonists made to use up leftovers. You can make this delicious dish too. You will need leftover chicken, a can of chicken bouillon, onions, potatoes, carrots, corn, peas, two pie crusts, a sharp knife, a cutting board, and a pan.

First, set out the pie crusts to thaw. Then cut the chicken into bite-sized pieces. Next, chop up the onions, carrots, and potatoes. Pour the chicken bouillon into the pan and heat it to boiling. Now add the vegetables and chicken and cook until the vegetables are tender.

Pour the mixture into one crust. Carefully place the other crust upside-down on the first crust. Press the edges firmly to seal the two. Bake the pie at 375°F for an hour or until the crust is golden brown. Now enjoy a colonial feast!

1. The first sentence puts the recipe in a context.
2. The second sentence clearly states the task.
3. Time-order words help show order of steps.
4. Adverbs and adjectives give specific details.
5. The ending connects back to the historical context.

# Writing a Compare/Contrast Essay

A **test** may ask you to write a compare/contrast essay. Choose subjects that are alike and different. Follow the tips below.

**Understand the prompt.** Read the prompt carefully. A prompt for a compare/contrast essay could look like this:

> Compare and contrast two real people or fictional characters, their lives, and their accomplishments. Tell about important similarities and differences.

Key words are *compare, contrast, lives, accomplishments, similarities,* and *differences.*

**Find a good topic.** Choose two people or characters you can compare and contrast in several ways.

**Organize your ideas.** Make a Venn diagram. Write differences in the outer parts of the circles and similarities in the center.

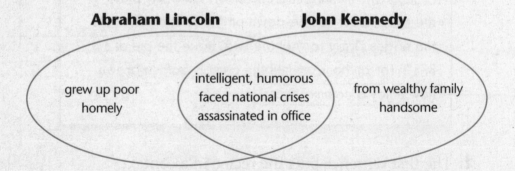

**Abraham Lincoln**          **John Kennedy**

grew up poor
homely

intelligent, humorous
faced national crises
assassinated in office

from wealthy family
handsome

**Write a good beginning.** Begin with a strong topic sentence.

**Develop and elaborate ideas.** Use the details in your diagram.

**Write a strong ending.** Use the ending to restate the main idea.

**Check your work.** Did you signal comparisons and contrasts?

See how the compare/contrast essay below addresses the prompt.

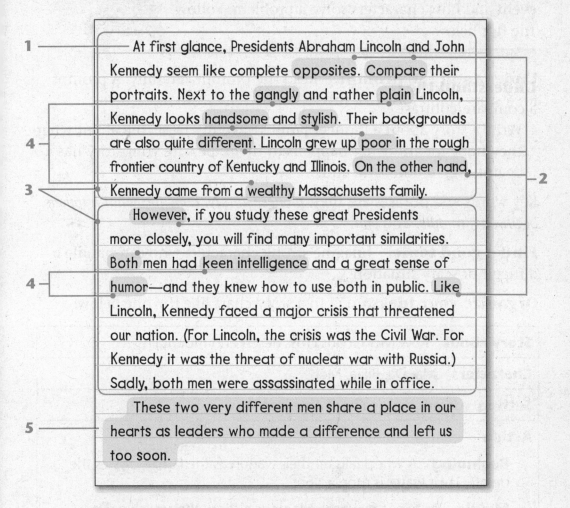

1 — At first glance, Presidents Abraham Lincoln and John Kennedy seem like complete opposites. Compare their portraits. Next to the gangly and rather plain Lincoln, Kennedy looks handsome and stylish. Their backgrounds are also quite different. Lincoln grew up poor in the rough frontier country of Kentucky and Illinois. On the other hand, Kennedy came from a wealthy Massachusetts family.

However, if you study these great Presidents more closely, you will find many important similarities. Both men had keen intelligence and a great sense of humor—and they knew how to use both in public. Like Lincoln, Kennedy faced a major crisis that threatened our nation. (For Lincoln, the crisis was the Civil War. For Kennedy it was the threat of nuclear war with Russia.) Sadly, both men were assassinated while in office.

These two very different men share a place in our hearts as leaders who made a difference and left us too soon.

1. The first sentence tells who will be compared.
2. The writer uses signal words throughout essay.
3. The writer organizes differences, then similarities.
4. Pairs of words clarify likenesses and differences.
5. The ending sums up the essay's main points.

# Writing a Story

A **test** may ask you to write a story. Tell about an event and how characters solve a problem. Follow the tips below.

**Understand the prompt.**   Read the prompt carefully. A prompt for a story could look like this:

> Write a story about a pioneer family traveling west. Tell about what they hope for and what happens to them. Be sure your story has a beginning, middle, and end.

Key words and phrases are *story, pioneer family, hope for, what happens, beginning, middle,* and *end.*

**Find a good topic.**   Imagine strong characters who can handle a difficult or scary situation.

**Organize your ideas.**   Fill in a story chart like the one below.

| | |
|---|---|
| **Story about**   how McKernans cross desert and mountains | |
| **Characters**   Ma, Da, Billie, Mol | |
| **Setting**   desert, mountains of American West | |
| **Action** | |
| **Beginning**   A wheel falls off their wagon as the family crosses the desert. Their water is running out. | |
| **Middle**   Da fixes the wheel; Ma sings a song; they reach a river, then cross mountains; they have to walk and help the horses; Ma must leave her good dishes and chest. | |
| **End**   They reach California. | |

**Write a good beginning.**   Introduce the characters, setting, and situation at the beginning.

**Develop and elaborate ideas.** Use your chart to organize events. Include vivid, specific words to bring events to life.

**Write a strong ending.** Show how the problem was resolved.

**Check your work.** Decide if anything needs to be changed.

See how the story below addresses the prompt.

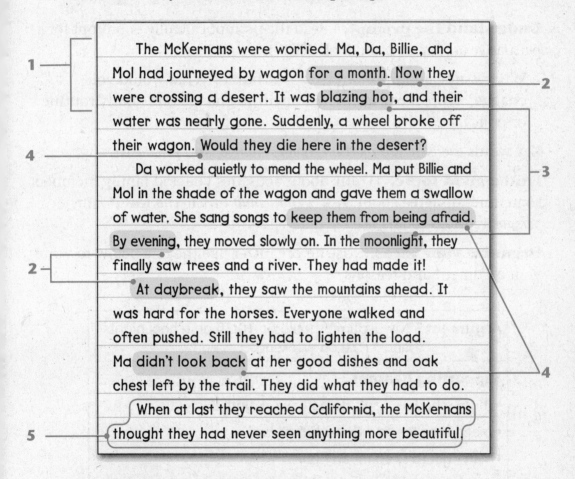

1 — The McKernans were worried. Ma, Da, Billie, and Mol had journeyed by wagon for a month. Now they were crossing a desert. It was blazing hot, and their water was nearly gone. Suddenly, a wheel broke off their wagon. Would they die here in the desert?

Da worked quietly to mend the wheel. Ma put Billie and Mol in the shade of the wagon and gave them a swallow of water. She sang songs to keep them from being afraid. By evening, they moved slowly on. In the moonlight, they finally saw trees and a river. They had made it!

At daybreak, they saw the mountains ahead. It was hard for the horses. Everyone walked and often pushed. Still they had to lighten the load. Ma didn't look back at her good dishes and oak chest left by the trail. They did what they had to do.

When at last they reached California, the McKernans thought they had never seen anything more beautiful.

**1.** The writer quickly introduces characters and setting.
**2.** The writer reports events in time order.
**3.** Vivid words set the scene and mood.
**4.** The writer shows characters' feelings.
**5.** The ending tells that the challenge was met.

# Writing a Persuasive Argument

A **test** may ask you to write a persuasive argument.
Support your ideas with examples, reasons, and language
that can convince a reader. Follow the tips below.

**Understand the prompt.** Read the prompt carefully. A prompt for a
persuasive argument could look like this:

> What issues are important to you at home? What would you
> change? Write a persuasive argument to change one family routine
> or policy.

Key words are *issues, important, home, change,* and *persuasive.*

**Find a good topic.** Think about activities you and family members
sometimes disagree about. Ask: *What could I try to change? What
persuasive words could I use?*

**Organize your ideas.** Use an organizer like the one below to write
your argument and reasons.

| | |
|---|---|
| **Argument** | My bedtime should be 10:30 on school nights and 11:30 on weekends. |

**Supporting Reasons**
- busy schedule, can't do homework until 8
- need time to wind down before bed
- can't get to sleep for an hour
- eight hours recommended amount of sleep

**Write a good beginning.** Set the tone for your argument.

**Develop and elaborate ideas.** Use your chart to focus your writing. Present the reasons using persuasive language.

**Write a strong ending.** Make the ending convincing.

**Check your work.** Have you supported your argument?

See how the persuasive argument below addresses the prompt.

1 —

Time is a valuable resource, and I never have enough. A 9:30 P.M. bedtime almost guarantees I won't be able to get everything done. Extending that time to 10:30 on school nights and 11:30 on weekends would make life less stressful.

With my after-school activities, I don't get to my homework before 8:00, and it usually takes more than an hour. Then right away I have to get ready for bed. When I lie down, my mind is still racing. I lie there wide awake for at least an hour. That is wasted time.

3 —

Studies show a person should spend some time winding down before trying to sleep. If I had an hour to play a game, watch TV, or listen to music, I could go right to sleep.

4 —

Doctors recommend getting eight hours of sleep a night. I have been spending nine and a half hours in bed. The later bedtime would give me enough rest and

5 —

relieve the stress of hurrying to get everything done.

2 —

1. The first sentence sets a brisk, straightforward tone.
2. The writer uses persuasive words effectively.
3. Varied sentence structures make writing flow smoothly.
4. The argument builds to the most important reason.
5. A strong ending sums up the writer's thoughts.

# Writing a Summary

A **test** may ask you to summarize information from a chart, diagram, or time line. You will need to read the information carefully and use it to develop your own sentences.

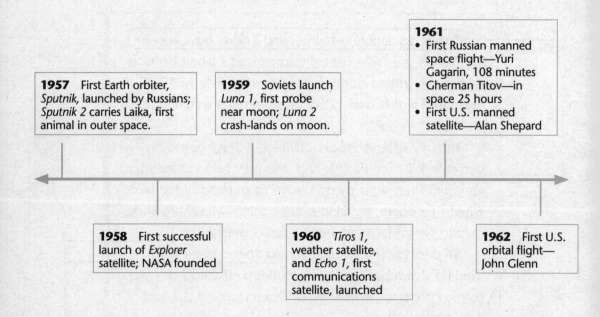

**1957** First Earth orbiter, *Sputnik,* launched by Russians; *Sputnik 2* carries Laika, first animal in outer space.

**1959** Soviets launch *Luna 1,* first probe near moon; *Luna 2* crash-lands on moon.

**1961**
• First Russian manned space flight—Yuri Gagarin, 108 minutes
• Gherman Titov—in space 25 hours
• First U.S. manned satellite—Alan Shepard

**1958** First successful launch of *Explorer* satellite; NASA founded

**1960** *Tiros 1,* weather satellite, and *Echo 1,* first communications satellite, launched

**1962** First U.S. orbital flight— John Glenn

**Organize your ideas.** Present the information from the time line in complete sentences. Use transition words and phrases such as *soon after* and *then* to show the order of events.

**Write a good beginning.** Write a topic sentence that states the main idea you want to present about your subject.

**Develop and elaborate ideas.** Include all important facts from the time line. Connect the ideas for your reader.

**Write a strong ending.** End with a comment of your own.

**Check your work.** Is your summary accurate?

See how the summary below is based on the time line.

---

### The Race for Space: 1957–1962

1 — Space exploration began as a race between the United States and the Soviet Union. In 1957, the Russians led with Sputnik, the first Earth orbiter, and — 2 Sputnik 2, which made the dog Laika the first animal in space. A year later, the U.S. launched an Explorer 3 — satellite and founded NASA.

In 1959, Luna 1, another Soviet satellite, was the first probe to go near the moon. Soon after, Luna 2 crash-landed on the moon. The next year, the — 3 U.S. sent up the weather satellite, Tiros 1, and the first communications satellite, Echo 1.

Yuri Gagarin made the first Russian manned space flight in 1961. He remained in flight for 108 minutes. Another Russian, Gherman Titov, was in space for 25 hours. The U.S. met the challenge with its own manned satellite with Alan Shepard. Then, in 1962, we claimed — 4 3 — our first manned orbital flight with John Glenn. I 4 — believe that the rivalry between the two countries made 5 — space exploration move ahead by leaps and bounds.

---

**1.** The opening paragraph clearly states the main idea.

**2.** The writer explains what *Sputnik* is.

**3.** Transition words and phrases show order of events.

**4.** Pronouns help avoid repetition.

**5.** The ending sums up main idea and reveals writer's voice.

# Grammar Patrol

# Grammar Patrol

**adjective**   An adjective describes a noun or a pronoun.

Ponds are *active* places.
*Several* chipmunks run through the *wet* grass.

Adjectives have two different forms that are used to make comparisons.

- Use the *–er* form of an adjective to compare two persons, places, or things.

    Frogs have *smoother* skin than toads.

- Use the *–est* form of an adjective to compare three or more persons, places, or things.

    Snails are the *slowest* pond creatures.

- The words *more* and *most* are often used with adjectives of two or more syllables to make comparisons.

    The ducks were *more comical* than usual.
    The goose is the *most common* bird here.

- Some adjectives show comparison in a special way. The correct forms of *good*, *bad*, *much*, and *little* are shown below.

| *good* weather | *better* weather | *best* weather |
| *bad* storm | *worse* storm | *worst* storm |
| *much* snow | *more* snow | *most* snow |
| *little* fog | *less* fog | *least* fog |

**article**   The words *a*, *an*, and *the* are a special kind of adjective. They are called articles. *The* is used with both singular and plural nouns. *A* and *an* are used only with singular nouns.

*The* animals at *the* pond are very busy.
*A* friend and I spent *an* afternoon there.

- Use *a* before a word that begins with a consonant sound.

    *a* beaver          *a* pleasant afternoon

- Use *an* before a word that begins with a vowel sound.

    *an* owl          *an* underwater plant

**adverb**   A word that describes a verb is an adverb.

- Some adverbs answer the question "How?"

  The fox hides *slyly* behind the bushes. (how?)

- Some adverbs answer the question "Where?"

  Aesop wrote fables *here*. (where?)

- Other adverbs answer the question "When?"

  *Often* a fable tells about one event. (when?)

Adverbs can be used to compare actions.

- Use the *-er* form or *more* to compare two actions. Most adverbs that end in *-ly* use *more*.

  The ant worked *harder* than the cricket.
  The tortoise moved *more steadily* than the hare.

- Use the *-est* form or *most* to compare three or more actions. Most adverbs that end in *-ly* use *most*.

  The ant worked *hardest* of all the insects.
  The tortoise moved *most steadily* of all.

The word *not* is an adverb. It means "no." Do not use two words that mean "no" in the same sentence.

  Wrong: It *wouldn't never* matter to me.
  Right: It *wouldn't* ever matter to me.
  Right: It would *never* matter to me.

**contraction**   A contraction is a shortened form of two words. An apostrophe replaces a letter or letters.

- Some contractions join a pronoun and a verb.

  *I have* never been in a dairy shed before.
  *I've* never been in a dairy shed before.

- Some contractions are formed from a verb and the word *not*.

  I *cannot* believe you *did not* bring your banjo.
  I *can't* believe you *didn't* bring your banjo.

**noun**   A noun names a person, place, or thing.

The *settlers* came to *America* on a *ship*.
(person)            (place)          (thing)

A **singular noun** names one person, place, or thing.

The *settler* kept the *cow* in the *barn*.

A **plural noun** names more than one person, place, or thing.

The *settlers* kept their *cows* in their *barns*.

• Add *-s* to form the plural of most nouns.

colonist**s**          river**s**                    pea**s**          chicken**s**

• Add *-es* to form the plural of nouns that end in *ch, sh, s, ss, x*, or *z*.

bench**es**          bush**es**                  bus**es**          box**es**

• If a noun ends in a consonant and *y*, change *y* to *i* and add *-es* to form the plural.

Singular:   library         city              cherry
Plural:      librar**ies**      cit**ies**         cherr**ies**

• Some plurals are formed by changing the spelling of the singular noun.

Singular:   man            child            foot          mouse
Plural:      m**e**n            child**ren**         f**ee**t         m**i**ce

• A few nouns have the same singular and plural forms.

Singular:   elk             moose           deer          sheep
Plural:      elk             moose           deer          sheep

A **common noun** names any person, place, or thing.

A *colonist* founded the *town*.

A **proper noun** names a particular person, place, or thing.

*William Penn* founded *Philadelphia*.

A **possessive noun** shows ownership.

- To form the possessive of a singular noun, add an apostrophe and s ('s) to the singular noun.

    *Ben Franklin's* many talents amazed people.

- To form the possessive of a plural noun ending in s, add an apostrophe (s').

    *shoemakers'* hammers         *blacksmiths'* forges

- To form the possessive of a plural noun that does not end in s, add an apostrophe and s ('s).

    *men's* hats     *mice's* tails     two *deer's* tracks

**preposition**    A preposition is a word that shows how a noun or pronoun is related to other words in the same sentence.

    We sing *in* the car.

A preposition begins a group of words called a **prepositional phrase**. At the end of the phrase is a noun or pronoun called the **object of the preposition**.

    Preposition: The dog buried its bone *in* the yard.
    Prepositional phrase: *in the yard*
    Object of the proposition: *yard*

**pronoun**    A pronoun takes the place of a noun or nouns.

    Nouns: *Linda* writes *poems.*
    Pronouns: *She* enjoys writing *them.*

The pronouns *I, you, she, he, it, we,* and *they* are **subject pronouns**. Use these pronouns to replace nouns that are the subjects of sentences.

    *Robert Frost* had been a teacher and a farmer.
    *He* wrote many poems about nature.

The pronouns *me, you, him, her, it, us,* and *them* are **object pronouns**. You can use these pronouns to replace nouns in the predicate of a sentence.

> Paul read *poems* to *Jill*.
> Paul read *them* to *her*.

The pronouns *my, your, his, her, its, our,* and *their* are **possessive pronouns**. A possessive pronoun shows ownership. Possessive pronouns can replace nouns.

> That *writer's* home is in the mountains.
> *Her* poems usually involve nature.

**sentence**   A sentence is a group of words that expresses a complete thought.

> *People of all ages enjoy hobbies.*

A **declarative sentence** makes a statement. It ends with a period (.).

> *Hobbies are important in people's lives.*

An **interrogative sentence** asks a question. It ends with a question mark (?).

> *What is your hobby?*

An **imperative sentence** gives a command or makes a request. It usually ends with a period (.).

> *Please get your kite ready.*        *Come to our party!*

An **exclamatory sentence** expresses strong feeling. It ends with an exclamation mark (!).

> *That kite will crash!*        *How happy I am!*

A **simple sentence** has one subject and one predicate. It expresses one complete thought.

> *Kites come in many different shapes.*

A **compound sentence** contains two simple sentences joined by the word *and, but,* or *or.* Use a comma in a compound sentence before the word *and, but,* or *or.*

>  *The day was cool*, and *clouds drifted across the sun.*

**subject and predicate** The subject is the part of the sentence that names someone or something. The predicate tells what the subject is or does. Both the subject and the predicate may be one word or many words.

>  *Currents/move ocean water around the world.*
>  *The most common mineral/is salt.*
>  *Ocean water/moves.*
>  *Sea water/flows in vast streams.*

The **simple subject** is the main word in the complete subject.

>  The five biggest *oceans* are really one huge ocean.

A sentence may have more than one simple subject. The word *and* may be used to join simple subjects, making a **compound subject**. The simple subjects share the same predicate.

>  Spiny *crabs* and colorful *fish* scurry along the underwater reef.

The **simple predicate** is the main word or words in the complete predicate.

>  Ocean waters *flow* in vast streams.

A sentence may have more than one simple predicate. The word *and* may be used to join simple predicates, making a **compound predicate**. The simple predicates share the same subject.

>  Some worms *live* and *feed* in the ocean.

**verb**   A verb is a word that shows action or being.

>  Nina *paints* in art class. (action)
>  That picture *is* beautiful. (being)

An **action verb** shows action. It tells what the subject of a sentence does.

> The art teacher *welcomed* the students.

A verb can be more than one word. The **main verb** is the most important verb. A **helping verb** works with the main verb.

> Many people have *admired* Picasso's paintings. (main verb)
> His name *is* known all over the world. (helping verb)

A **linking verb** shows being. It tells what the subject is or was.

> Grandma Moses *was* a famous artist.

When the correct subject and verb are used together, we say they agree. The form of the linking verb *be* that is used depends on the subject of the sentence. Study the following chart.

### Using the Forms of *be*

| | |
|---|---|
| Use *am* and *was* | with *I* |
| Use *is* and *was* | with *she, he, it,* and singular nouns |
| Use *are* and *were* | with *we, you, they,* and plural nouns |

The **tense** of a verb shows the time of the action.

A verb in the **present tense** shows action that happens now.

> Eli *forms* the tiles.

A verb in the present tense must agree with the subject of the sentence.

- With *he, she, it,* or a singular noun, add *-s* or *-es* to the verb.

  > The student learn*s*.    My cousin teach*es*.    He walk*s*.

- If a verb ends in *ch, sh, s, ss, x,* or *z,* add *-es*. Notice the word *teaches* above.

- With *I, you, we, they,* or a plural noun, do not add *-s* or *-es*.

  > The students learn.    My cousins teach.    They walk.

A verb in the **future tense** shows action that will happen. The future tense is formed with the helping verb *will*.

> Ann *will create* a vase.

A verb in the **past tense** shows action that already happened.

> Lee *washed* pots.

The past tenses of irregular verbs are not formed by adding *-ed*. Some irregular verbs are shown in the following chart.

| Verb | Past | Past with *have, has,* or *had* |
|------|------|------|
| begin | began | begun |
| bring | brought | brought |
| come | came | come |
| do | did | done |
| eat | ate | eaten |
| fall | fell | fallen |
| find | found | found |
| fly | flew | flown |
| give | gave | given |
| go | went | gone |
| grow | grew | grown |
| ride | rode | ridden |
| run | ran | run |
| see | saw | seen |
| take | took | taken |
| throw | threw | thrown |
| write | wrote | written |

The spelling of some verbs changes when *-es* or *-ed* is added.

- If a verb ends in a consonant and *y*, change the *y* to *i* before adding *-es* or *-ed*.

  | | | |
  |------|------|------|
  | study | stud*ies* | stud*ied* |

- If a verb ends in one vowel and one consonant, double the final consonant before adding *-ed*.

  | | | | |
  |------|------|------|------|
  | trap | tra*pped* | stir | sti*rred* |

# Capitalization

**first word of a sentence**   Every sentence begins with a capital letter.

>*People* enjoy having special projects.

**proper noun**   Each important word in a proper noun begins with a capital letter.

- Capitalize each word in the name of a person or pet.

  >*Patrice Gomez* owns a cat named *Duke*.

- Capitalize an initial in a name. Put a period after the initial.

  >William *L.* Chen is a doctor in our neighborhood.

- Capitalize a title before a name. If the title is an *abbreviation* (a shortened form of a word), put a period after it.

  >*President* Jefferson        *Dr.* Jonas Salk

- Capitalize every important word in the names of particular places or things.

  >*Statue of Liberty*        *Ellis Island*        *New York Harbor*

- Capitalize names of days, months, holidays, and special days.

  >*Tuesday*                *April*            *Fourth of July*

**pronoun *I***   The pronoun *I* is always capitalized.

>May *I* go skating this afternoon?

**letter**   Capitalize the first word of the greeting and the first word of the closing of a letter.

>*Dear* Mother,            *Dear* Sir:            *Sincerely* yours,

**title of books, movies, songs, and other works**   Capitalize the first word, the last word, and all of the important words in the titles of works.

>The Secret Life of Harold the Bird Watcher
>"The Star-Spangled Banner"

**quotation**   Begin the first word in a quotation with a capital letter.

> The Hare asked, "*How* about a race?"

## Punctuation

**period**   Declarative sentences and imperative sentences end with a period (.).

> *I stood on the corner.*       *Wait for the signal.*

• Put a period after an initial in a name.

> J. P. Jones                Abigail S. Adams

• Put a period after an abbreviation (a shortened form of a word).

> *Mr.*       *Mrs.*        *Ms.*              *Dr.*

**question mark**   An interrogative sentence ends with a question mark (?).

> *Do you have more than one hobby?*

**exclamation mark**   An exclamatory sentence ends with an exclamation mark (!).

> *That kite will crash!*

**comma**   A comma (,) is a signal that tells a reader to pause.

• Use a comma after *yes*, *no*, or *well* at the beginning of a sentence.

> *Yes*, I saw the display of Eskimo art.
> *Well*, my favorites were the bears made of silver.

• Use a comma to set off the name of the person spoken to.

> *Your painting is very beautiful, Roberta.*

• Use a comma to separate words in a series. A series is made up of three or more items. No comma is used after the last word in the series. The last comma goes before the word *and*.

> *The artists carve, smooth, and polish their work.*

- Use a comma to separate the city from the state.

  I grew up in *Tulsa, Oklahoma.*

- Use a comma to separate the day and the year.

  Pablo was born on *February 7, 2000.*

- Use a comma after the greeting of a friendly letter. Use a comma after the closing of a friendly or a business letter.

  *Dear Kim,*      *Your friend,*      *Yours truly,*

- Use a comma before the word *and*, *but*, or *or* in a compound sentence.

  **The merchants crossed central Asia, and they reached China.**

**quotation marks**   A quotation is the exact words someone speaks. Quotation marks (" ") show where a speaker's exact words begin and end.

- Use quotation marks before and after a quotation. Begin the first word in a quotation with a capital letter. When the quotation comes last, use a comma to separate the speaker from the quotation.

  The Tortoise said, "I'm not going to lose this race."

- When the quotation comes first, use a comma, a question mark, or an exclamation mark to separate the quotation from the speaker. The end mark of a quotation always comes just before the second quotation mark. Put a period at the end of the sentence.

  Statement: "Let's do something else," replied the Tortoise.
  Question: "Are you afraid you'll lose?" teased the Hare.
  Exclamation: "I'm not afraid!" snapped the Tortoise.

- Enclose the titles of stories, songs, poems, and articles in quotation marks.

  Story: "The Use of Force"
  Song: "Of Thee I Sing"
  Poem: "Dear March, Come In!"
  Article: "Let's Make Music"

- Underline the titles of newspapers, magazines, books, plays, and movies.

  In materials you read, these titles are printed in italics.

  *Newspaper:* <u>Denver Post</u>
  *Magazine:* <u>Popular Mechanics</u>
  *Book:* <u>A Wind in the Door</u>
  *Play:* <u>Man of La Mancha</u>
  *Movie:* <u>Invaders from Mars</u>

**apostrophe**   Use an apostrophe (') to show where a letter or letters have been left out in a *contraction* (a shortened form of two words).

  *we've* (we + have)     *wasn't* (was + not)

- Use an apostrophe to form the possessive of a noun.

  *man's*        *James's*         *men's*          *workers'*

**colon**   Use a colon (:) after the greeting in a business letter.

  *Dear Mr. Kurtz:*        *Dear Sir or Madam:*

# Frequently Misspelled Words

| | | | |
|---|---|---|---|
| a lot | everything | morning | then |
| afraid | except | myself | there |
| again | excited | of | they |
| almost | family | off | they're |
| already | favorite | once | thought |
| always | February | one | through |
| another | field | opened | to |
| are | finally | our | too |
| athlete | first | outside | took |
| basketball | found | people | tries |
| beautiful | friend | piece | truly |
| because | getting | presents | TV |
| before | government | pretty | two |
| believe | grabbed | probably | until |
| brother | happened | radio | upon |
| brought | heard | really | usually |
| buy | hero | right | vacation |
| caught | his | said | very |
| chocolate | hospital | scared | want |
| Christmas | house | school | was |
| clothes | I | separate | watch |
| control | I'm | should | weird |
| could | instead | since | went |
| cousin | into | sincerely | we're |
| Dad's | it's | something | were |
| decided | knew | sometimes | what |
| didn't | know | special | when |
| different | knowledge | started | where |
| disappear | let's | stopped | which |
| doesn't | library | successful | who |
| don't | little | sure | whole |
| enough | maybe | surprised | with |
| especially | might | swimming | would |
| everybody | minute | that's | you're |
| everyone | Mom | their | |

# D'Nealian™ Alphabet

ā b c d ē f g h i

j k l m n ō p q r s t

u v w x y z

A B C D E F G

H I J K L M N O

P Q R S T U V

W X Y Z . , ' ?

1 2 3 4 5 6

7 8 9 10

# Manuscript Alphabet

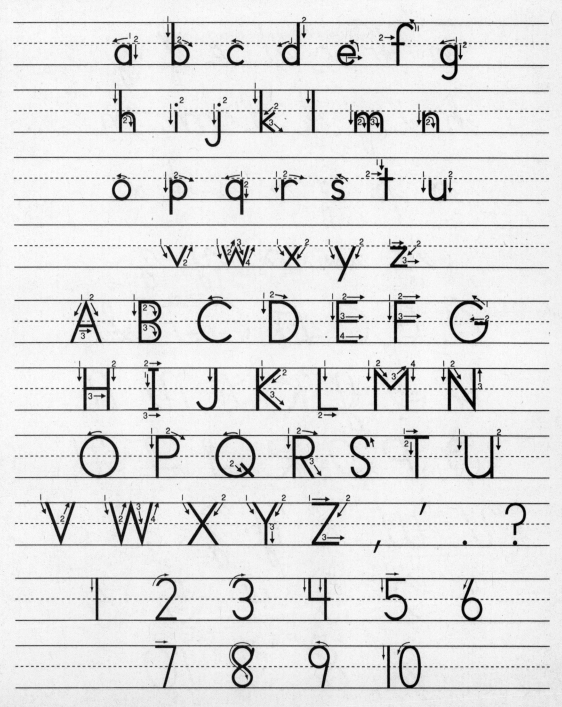

# Cursive Alphabet

a b c d e f g
h i j k l m n
o p q r s t u
v w x y z

A B C D E F G
H I J K L M N
O P Q R S T U
V W X Y Z . , ' ?

1 2 3 4 5 6
7 8 9 10

# Index

# Index

# Index

indefinite, 158–161

object, 140–143

possessive, 152–155

referents, 146–149

reflexive, 158–161

subject, 140–143

*who* and *whom,* 164–167

**Proofreading,** 22–25

**Proper adjectives.** *See* Adjectives.

**Proper nouns.** *See* Nouns.

**Punctuation,** 50–53, 62–65, 68–71, 74–77, 86–89, 170–173, 212–215, 218–221, 224–227, 254–256 *See also* Mechanics.

**Purpose for writing,** 2–3, 168

## Q

**Question mark,** 50–53

**Quotation marks,** 218–221

**Quotations,** 218–221

## R

**Referents.** *See* Antecedents.

**Reflexive pronouns.** *See* Pronouns.

**Review,** 53, 59, 65, 71, 77, 83, 89, 95, 101, 107, 113, 119, 125, 131, 137, 143, 149, 155, 161, 167, 173, 179, 185, 191, 197, 203, 209, 215, 221, 227

**Rubrics,** 26, 31, 36, 41

**Run-on sentences,** 56–59

## S

**Semicolon,** 224–227

**Sentences,** 18–21, 249–250

capitalization in, 50–53

complex, 62–65, 68–71, 206–209

compound, 68–71, 206–209

compound-complex, 68–71

declarative, 50–53

exclamatory, 50–53

imperative, 50–53

interrogative, 50–53

kinds of, 50–53

punctuation of, 50–53

run-on, 56–59

simple, 68–71

**Simile,** 186

**Simple sentences.** *See* Sentences.

**Spelling,** 257

**Strategies.** *See* Writing.

**Subject complements,** 122–125

**Subject pronouns.** *See* Pronouns.

**Subjects,** 250

complete, 56–59

compound, 206–209

plural, 98–101

simple, 56–59

singular, 98–101

## T

## V

## W

# Index